THE BIG *SQUEEZE*

Balancing the Needs of Aging Parents, Dependent Children, and YOU

Barbara A. Shapiro, Ph.D.

with

Vicki Konover, M.S.
and
Ann Shapiro, M.A.

Mills & Sanderson, Publishers
Bedford, MA • 1991

DISCLAIMER

The majority of the vignettes and examples used in this book are based on the life situations of actual people experiencing the squeeze of living in the sandwich generation. The names and specifics have been changed to insure anonymity and confidentiality.

Published by Mills & Sanderson, Publishers
41 North Road, Suite 201 • Bedford, MA 01730

Library of Congress Cataloging-in-Publication Data

Shapiro, Barbara A., 1951-
The big squeeze : balancing the needs of aging parents, dependent children, and you / Barbara A. Shapiro with Vicki Konover and Ann Shapiro.
p. cm.
Includes bibliographical references and index.
ISBN 0-938179-29-22 : $12.95
1. Aging parents--Care--United States. 2. Aging parents--United States--Family relationships. 3. Adult children--United States--Psychology. I. Konover, Vicki. II. Shapiro, Ann. III. Title.
HQ1063.6.S53 1991
306.874--dc20 91-18195
CIP

Printed and manufactured by Capital City Press.
Cover design by Lyrl Ahern.

Printed and Bound in the United States of America

To our parents, in-laws, children, and husbands

ACKNOWLEDGMENT

We want to thank Dr. Joseph Luft for permission to use the Johari Window in this book. The Johari Window, and information pertaining to it, appeared in *Of Human Interaction*, Mayfield Publishing, © 1969.

♦ Contents ♦

SECTION I

Before You Begin

Does The Big Squeeze Have You In Its Grasp?

It's Not Just Your Mother ... Daughter ... Job ...

"I feel like such a witch," Carol Brayman said. "Nothing's even happened yet and already I'm getting my appointments all confused, I'm screaming at the kids—and Steven—I've been so awful to Steven, and he's the one with the real problem; it's *his* mother."

The *nothing* that has happened is that Carol's mother-in-law, a self-sufficient and healthy—but slightly arthritic—75-year-old woman, has moved to town. The *nothing* that has happened is that Carol's Big Squeeze has begun.

* * * *

Despite years of saving for their children's college education, Linda and Dave Spinelli found they could not save enough. Even after their eldest daughter Elizabeth had applied for and received every possible scholarship and loan, Linda was still forced to change from part-time to full-time work, Dave to seriously consider moonlighting, and Elizabeth to take on an evening job while at the university. Linda, Dave, Elizabeth, and the three younger children decided the sacrifices were worth it.

Then, in the fall of Elizabeth's freshman year, Dave's father suffered a series of strokes and was in need of considerable custodial care. He denied his need, and refused to enter a nursing home or to spend his life's savings on in-home care he proclaimed to be unnecessary.

Dave felt responsible for helping his father through this difficult time, and he and Linda decided to pay for the aide his father so obviously needed—even though Mr. Spinelli only grudgingly allowed the woman into his house, and even though Dave found his feelings of worry were now sometimes accompanied by anger and resentment—along with a strong dose of guilt.

The Spinelli's Big Squeeze has also begun. They survived the first month of Dave's father's illness, when Dave spent all his time at the hospital or on the phone with his two sisters in California, but Dave and Linda don't know how they are going to survive the financial squeeze the elderly man's lingering illness is going to cause. The reality of the Big Squeeze is that it does not only squeeze once; it squeezes many times, for many years.

* * * *

It was past 10:00 when Susan Hagan's 4-year-old son finally fell asleep, semi-convinced that dinosaurs don't eat little boys—but that if they did his mother would chase them away. Exhausted, Susan climbed into bed, but was awakened within an hour by her father, who called to confide a worry he had been keeping from her; he had heard that his apartment was turning condo at the end of the month, and he had nowhere to go. Susan calmed his fears and told him not to worry, to get some sleep, that she would handle the entire affair.

Susan's father did exactly as his daughter suggested and was soon fast asleep; Susan spent the remainder of the night wide awake, worrying about where she was ever going to find an apartment he could afford, and where she was ever going to find the time to look for it.

"Sure my father could sleep," Susan said to a friend the next day, "he doesn't have a problem any more. I have it—and it's sitting right here in *my* lap!"

But Susan should not blame her father because his problem was in her lap; she was the one who allowed it to settle there. She could have offered to help in any number of ways—to give him the name of an attorney to determine his legal rights, to get him in touch with the Senior Center Listing Service to check on senior housing options, to help him go over newspaper listings, or to drive him to see apartments. Instead, she took complete responsibility for her father's problem—as well as its solution. Susan will soon discover that she has taken on more than simply finding her father an apartment—she has taken on the Big Squeeze.

* * * *

The Big Squeeze. Finding yourself inside that 1990's pressure cooker in which your daughter's dance recital pushes from below, your husband's job dissatisfaction pushes from your right, the memo that your boss wanted yesterday pushes from your left, your mother's doctor's appointment pushes from the top—and what about the seeds you were supposed to germinate for the garden club tomorrow night? Sound familiar? If it does—or even if you only have one-half of these things going on in your life, or even if you anticipate you will soon be in this situation, or even if you are only trying to help a friend with her problems—you have picked up the right book.

The Big Squeeze. The on-going, life-changing, energy-draining situation facing the sandwich generation: those squashed between the simultaneous and seemingly-endless demands of their aging parents and dependent children.

The Big Squeeze. The nemesis of the generation that thought they could have it all and do it all; that thought they could have family, career, and self-actualization; that never thought *family* included parents aging beyond the golf-tennis-retirement-with-gusto phase.

The Big Squeeze. Can you make it go away? No. Can you survive it? Yes.

How Did You Get Here?

You got here by virtue of reaching the middle portion of your life at this particular time, by virtue of being an adult child at the historical moment when:

- extended families are geographically dispersed;
- childbearing is often postponed;
- two-income families are becoming both the norm and a necessity;
- divorced and remarried families are commonplace;
- longevity is increasing;
- medical advances increase the elderly's period of dependency by allowing people to live longer—but often with more debilitating diseases;
- a wide gap exists between male and female life expectancy;
- there is a lower ratio of adult children to aging parents than ever before.

The family is changing. Work is changing. Life is changing. Death is changing. And you are caught in the middle, trying to adjust, cope, and juggle all the effects of these changes, while also struggling with the psychological, emotional, and physical issues of mid-life.

The changing family

Mobility, divorce, remarriage, working women, first-time mothers in their thirties and forties—all of these factors have had a profound effect on the American family. The family farm, the two- or three-family house shared by multiple generations, the stay-at-home mother caring for two children fathered by her current husband—these situations, so common a mere twenty or thirty years ago, are becoming more difficult to find. Remarried families, single parents, siblings and parents separated by thousands of miles, day-care centers and two-income households are more typical of contemporary family life.

Americans are marrying later: in 1950 the average age at first marriage was approximately 23 for men and 20 for women, in 1990 the numbers were 26 and 24 respectively. Americans are having children later: in the early 1970s, 4 percent of first children were born to mothers over 30, now the figure is approaching 20 percent. And we are having fewer children: the *typical* American family contained eight children in the late 1700s versus two children today. We are also divorcing more (roughly half of all first marriages end in divorce) and remarrying more (75–80 percent of divorcees remarry, with a second marriage failure rate of about 60 percent). These *reconstituted* families produce a bewildering array of step- and half-relationships which must be carefully navigated with little assistance from previous role models.

Women are entering the work place in greater and greater numbers: women account for 60 percent of the increase in the American labor force, and a whopping 71 percent of mothers with school-age children—and 60 percent of those with children under six—currently work outside the home. This creates three jobs—his, hers, and the household's —where before there were only two. Equal distribution of the household and family tasks adds 50 percent to each spouse's work load, while the more common alternative—women who fail to distribute their household and childcare tasks and/or men who fail to share them—creates a serious overload situation for the wife. For a society in which the care of aging parents has traditionally fallen to nonworking women, the fact that more than half of this pool of caretakers is also holding down a job has far-reaching effects.

A harried morning getting everyone out the door, followed by a full day of work, followed by a stop at the supermarket and a hastily prepared dinner, followed by baths or homework assistance, or bill-paying or laundry, is not an uncommon scenario for today's mid-life man or woman. And one need not have a traditional out-of-the-home, nine-to-five job to work every day: the woman who "works" at home, juggling the needs of three children, community responsibilities and a husband who travels half of every week, is just as harried as any "working" woman. It is easy to see why difficulties erupt when a needy elderly parent is added into this equation.

The changing facts of aging

A male child born in the United States in 1900 could expect to live 48 years, a male child born in 1940 could expect to live 61 years, and a male child born in 2060 will have a life expectancy of 77 years. This increasing longevity has caused two related demographic trends: the growth of the elderly (65 and over) as a proportion of the American population, and a rapid increase in the percentage of those who are very old (85 and over).

The proportion of elderly jumped from 4 percent in 1900 to over 12 percent in 1990, with expectations that almost a quarter of the population will be over 65 in the year 2050. Figures for the very old are even more staggering; from almost none in 1900 to over 1 percent of the American population in 1990, this group is expected to increase to close to 2 percent in 2000 and to be greater than 5 percent by the year 2050, when an estimated 16 million people will be over 85.

What do these longevity figures mean to you? They show you why there seem to be so many elders (parents, in-laws, step-parents, ex-in-laws, aunts, uncles) needing, or potentially needing, your care. They also show you something about the type and intensity of care needed, for the over-85 group requires the most extensive and expensive (in time, emotion, and dollars) care, and this group is also the fastest growing segment of our population.

And there's more. There's the fact that although many of the diseases that used to kill people young and quickly (i.e. smallpox, tuberculosis) have been eradicated or arrested, the common diseases of the elderly today (i.e. Alzheimer's, Parkinson's) often leave people in chronic disease states that, while allowing them to live into old age, erode their independence. There is the growing gap in life expectancy between men and women (especially apparent in the over-85 group) that strands many aging women without the day-to-day physical, emotional, and financial support they need. And there is the fact that the American birth rate has been decreasing, thereby reducing the number of potential caretakers just as the number of those needing care increases.

Mid-life changes

And then there's *you*: an individual in the middle segment of life, with diverse expectations, needs, and abilities, struggling to keep it all together as the world becomes increasingly complex and the demands upon you swell. Whether you are a man assessing your future career potential, a woman carving a new self after the nest empties, a mid-to-late thirties mother overwhelmed by two children, or a superwoman who appears to have it all, the Big Squeeze comes at a time when you could easily live without the additional burdens. For, on top of everything else, mid-life brings its own set of issues and dilemmas to be confronted and resolved.

It's been called middlescence, the middle years, middle age. Those entering it don't want to acknowledge it, and those leaving it don't want to part with it. It's said to be a time of maximum career productivity and a time of agonizing personal reassessment, a time when the first lessening of physical prowess becomes apparent amidst a widening of intellectual and creative potential. It's a time of matching youthful expectations to adult realities and possibilities—a time of turmoil, change, and growth.

You may be loathe to admit it, but if you are in the middle third of your life—with roughly half your life behind you and half in front of you—you are living in the middle. And if you have an elderly parent who needs your care, and children who still depend upon you, then you are living in the middle of the Big Squeeze.

It can happen fast ...

Brian and Noreen Porter had the perfect relationship with his parents. The elder Porters lived about three miles from Brian and Noreen, and each couple considered the other their friends as well as their family. The younger Porters were the recipients of much needed and appreciated loans and babysitting, and the elder Porters had their plants watered and house maintained when they travelled. The two families had dinner together frequently, spent a week together each summer at the beach, and generally enjoyed a balanced interdependency.

Well into her seventies, Brian's mother developed Parkinson's disease. She had trouble with her balance and moved slowly, but with the help of her husband and medication she managed quite nicely. The two families continued to enjoy their time together.

One night Brian's father suffered a massive coronary and died; within a month of the funeral his mother's condition had deteriorated to the point that her memory lapses, physical instability, and depression precluded her living alone.

Unprepared, and caught totally off-guard, Brian and Noreen were catapulted into the Big Squeeze.

... Or it can happen slow ...

Judith Houlihan was a single mother raising three children, with sporadic assistance from her ex-husband. Even though she knew she was overly dependent on her parents—who lived about an hour away—and even though she sometimes hated herself for it, she so badly needed support that she let herself fall into calling her parents when her teenage son got into trouble at school, when the toilet overflowed, or when she was being harassed by her boss. They came to her aid every time.

When Judith's father developed terminal cancer, both she and her mother were devastated. But the two women supported each other through the trauma of his illness and death, and ultimately both adjusted quite well. Mary Fitzgerald, a heathy, independent 74-year-old, became very active in her church and started to travel—something her husband had never wanted to do. Mother and daughter remained very close.

Over the next couple of years, it slowly dawned on Judith that her mother was slipping; even though it made her feel scared and vulnerable, she couldn't help noticing that Mrs. Fitzgerald's hearing and memory didn't seem to be what they had been, and that her mother was spending more and more time at home alone. Judith took her to the doctor and a spot on her lung was found to be malignant, but her age precluded surgery. The older woman became weaker and fell once in awhile, but refused either a caretaker or a nursing home.

After her mother fell and broke her wrist, Judith demanded that she move in with them. Mrs. Fitzgerald reluctantly agreed; the kids were thrilled and Judith was relieved. Although the older woman seemed happy to be in the house, she was resentful of the caretaker that Judith hired to come in when she was at work.

They stumbled along without any major problems until Mrs. Fitzgerald's sleep patterns became reversed and she began to sleep all day and be awake all night. Judith couldn't afford two caretakers, so she was forced to stay up most of the night to ensure that her mother didn't fall down the stairs or forget to turn off the stove.

Judith saw it coming, she had felt it grow slowly, but now she was really in the grip of the Big Squeeze.

... But it is NEVER a one shot deal

The Big Squeeze can come out of the blue (as in the case of Brian and Noreen Porter) or develop slowly over a period of many years (as in the case of Judith Houlihan), but it's almost never a one shot deal. By definition, the Big Squeeze is a long-term situation that requires long-term attention. It might be your mother-in-law's 8-year bout with Alzheimer's or your father's failing eyesight—or it might be both. It could be the heavy burdens of daily care for an elderly aunt in a wheelchair, or an almost imperceptibly increasing neediness in the mother you always considered self-sufficient.

The Big Squeeze isn't a single event, it's a series of little and big events—little and big squeezes that go on for years. It has been estimated that the average American woman spends seventeen years or more caring for her children, and eighteen years or more caring for elderly relatives. Your Big Squeeze is here—and it may well stick around for a decade or two.

What you need is a method of problem solving for all the years of squeezes ahead of you. You need to learn how to survive with your sanity and your family intact—for now and for the future, for yourself, for your children, for your spouse, and for your parents.

This book will teach you that method. It will help you to develop a better understanding of your situation and choices —and how to make the best of both. It will help you find the balance you need to negotiate the tightrope you are walking —and it will help you develop a safety net you can count on when that precarious balance is upset.

You Can Make It With A Little Bit Of Balance

Nancy Woicik was having a terrible day. Late that afternoon her boss had dumped two days worth of typing on her desk with ASAP stamped on every page. She got through over half of it, but she was late getting her daughter Stephanie from art class and her son Tim from soccer practice. Then, after throwing in a load of laundry and shoving the breakfast dishes into the dishwasher, she checked her answering machine and discovered that her mother had fallen and broken her hip. Distraught with worry and fatigue, Nancy spent a frantic hour on the phone before she finally reached her mother at the hospital.

Obviously, Nancy's day is yet another casualty of the Big Squeeze. But the important question now is whether Nancy is also a casualty.

It was almost two days before Stan Woicik was able to return from his business trip so that Nancy could go to her mother in Fort Lauderdale. After her first visit to the hospital, Nancy decided that her mother would have to come live with them, even though space would be tight.

It would be good for everyone to have three generations under one roof. Stephanie would move into the sewing room upstairs and Stan would build a ramp into the garage. The children would be thrilled to have their grandmother so close, and the older woman would enjoy watching her grandchildren grow.

Suffused with feelings of a job well-done, Nancy flew home to ready the house for her mother's arrival.

* * * *

Is Nancy a casualty of the Big Squeeze? She exhibited all the tell-tale signs:

- Making hasty—and solo—decisions in an emotional state;
- Making incorrect assumptions about her mother's wishes, needs, and expectations because of a lack of awareness of her mother as an individual with a life and desires of her own;
- Projecting her own feelings onto others because of a lack of communication with all the people affected;
- Failing to delegate;
- Perhaps most important, thinking that she had to, and could, handle it all by herself.

* * * *

Three months after Nancy's mother Helen moved in, her hip was healing nicely; she was able to get around with a walker and have meals with the family. But that was about all that was going nicely in the Woicik household.

Stephanie barely spoke to her grandmother and was rude when she did—incorrectly blaming Helen for stealing her room. Stan was unwilling to admit his annoyance with the amount of attention Nancy was lavishing on her mother, so instead he started volunteering for long-distance business trips more often than he had previously. Helen was bored and restless without her Florida friends, and, although she tried to hide it, her daughter often caught her staring sadly out the kitchen window.

Nancy was confused and miserable as she tried to deal with her morose daughter, her absent husband, and her obviously unhappy mother. Only Tim appeared oblivious to the changes.

* * * *

Nancy, for all her good intentions, has made some serious errors. Her biggest error was trying to do it all. Nancy could not handle this complex web of intergenerational needs and relationships by herself. And, most likely, neither can you—possibly no one can. Attempting to manage the Big Squeeze is not an easy undertaking, but given the number of years you will probably be there, it is something that is in your—and your family's—best interest to do.

Having a full life, filled with activities and responsibilities and many people to love and care for, is a wonderful thing. Being able to share your adulthood with your parents is also a wonderful thing; you all get to spend more years together, your children get to know their grandparents, and everyone reaps the benefits that come from a multigeneration, extended family.

But sometimes your commitments may demand more of your time and energy than you planned. Sometimes your children may grow and develop in unlikely directions. Sometimes your parents may age in a manner you didn't anticipate. And sometimes, it all seems to happen at the same time: suddenly everyone is demanding of you, everyone needs you, and they all need you in ways you never imagined—or planned for. You may feel poked, prodded, pulled, and squeezed. You may feel like you are walking a tightrope without a net—and you may feel like you are on the verge of losing your balance.

So what can you do? How can you handle it? How can you possibly manage to stay upright?

You can find your balance by developing a new and flexible way of coping that will allow you to recognize and adapt to the on-going and future stresses in your life. You can find your balance by cultivating skills that will enhance the coping abilities you already have, but that are geared toward the specifics of your particular situation. You can find your balance by learning an active problem-solving method that will help you sort wishes from needs, recognize and evaluate what your choices are, and enable you and your family to carry out the actions you have collectively decided are best. If you can do these things, you will be able to find some balance; you will also be able to survive your Big Squeeze—in all its manifestations, for as many years as necessary.

This book describes a method, The Balancing Act, that can help you achieve this goal. It can help you avoid mistakes like Nancy's, because it will teach you how to use the available resources to get the support you need. The Balancing Act will help you see yourself and the situation more clearly, and will teach you to problem-solve in a rational manner that will include—and benefit—all those involved.

The Balancing Act's Background

The Balancing Act is a method that grew out of co-authors Vicki Konover and Ann Shapiro's experiences working with families of the elderly. They began to notice that they were seeing an increasing number of people who could be considered members of the "sandwich generation"—those caught between the competing demands of their dependent children and their aging parents. More and more often, the gerontologists were being asked for help by an adult child who still had emotional, financial or day-to-day responsibility for their children, while confronting a problem that was related to the needs of an elderly parent.

Having had considerable experience working with families of the elderly, Konover and Shapiro quickly recognized that for members of this group the challenges were different; these people's problems and crises were made even more difficult and complex by the stressful overload situation that existed in their lives. Practically, emotionally, and logistically, many of these men and women were overloaded by their ongoing family, work, and community responsibilities. When an aging parent was added to the picture, this overload often became too heavy to bear.

As a result, these adult children felt like they were not doing all they should, that they were not living up to their responsibilities, that they were failing—failing their parents, their children, and themselves. These feelings of failure often led to tremendous guilt, which further limited their ability to meet perceived responsibilities, and often spiraled them into a continuing cycle of failure, anxiety, anger, and guilt —followed by more failure, more anxiety, more anger, and more guilt.

It became apparent that until these adult children's feelings about their parents, their children, their careers, their guilt, and their expectations for themselves were addressed, there could be no long-lasting satisfaction for anyone involved. So Konover and Shapiro decided to broaden the focus, to go beyond the more traditional concern with the aging parent, and to include the adult child's issues—all the stresses and related feelings with which he or she was wrestling.

After years of doing both individual and group therapy with adult children dealing with aging parents, the gerontologists began to notice that the more successful ones seemed to follow a pattern. Although it wasn't always the *exact* same series of steps for each individual, an underlying progression of emotional and practical steps appeared to lead, in most cases, to more balance and satisfaction for the adult child, and better relationships with the important others in his or her life. These are the steps of The Balancing Act.

The Balancing Act Method

The Balancing Act focuses on increasing your awareness and acceptance of the emotional aspects (i.e. incomplete filial maturity, repaying the parental debt, needing to be needed, fear of death—your own and your parents') and the practical aspects (i.e. expectations, needs, resources) of being a member of this group. The goals are multiple:

- To help you achieve a more realistic view of your own, and your family members' needs, strengths, and limitations;
- To help you understand that there are reasonable limits to what you can expect from yourself, and that others are more capable than you might think;
- To help you understand the limits of everyone's control;
- To help you and your family see all your options and choices more clearly;
- To help you and your family take action on those options and choices;
- And ultimately, to help you and your family achieve a workable interdependence which will translate into a more balanced, less stressful life for everyone involved.

If there were easy solutions to your problems, you probably would have discovered them by now. The reason you haven't found any of those simple solutions is because there are none.

But the Balancing Act can help you deal with this solutionless situation; not by handing you simple answers, but by helping you understand what you are doing, and helping you explore what motivates your behavior. The Balancing Act will help you take positive action; not by telling you which actions to take, but by teaching you a method to help *you* figure out what *your* best options are.

Obviously, your situation is unique, and the practical and emotional help you need to achieve your own balance is unique; The Balancing Act recognizes this uniqueness and allows for it. For although the method is organized into a series of steps which follow one another, it is not necessary—in some cases not even preferable—for you to follow it exactly as it is organized.

The figure below shows The Balancing Act as an interconnected system of loops. It is an attempt to show you geometrically that The Balancing Act is really a circle, with loops and connections between all the steps, rather than a linear series of eight steps.

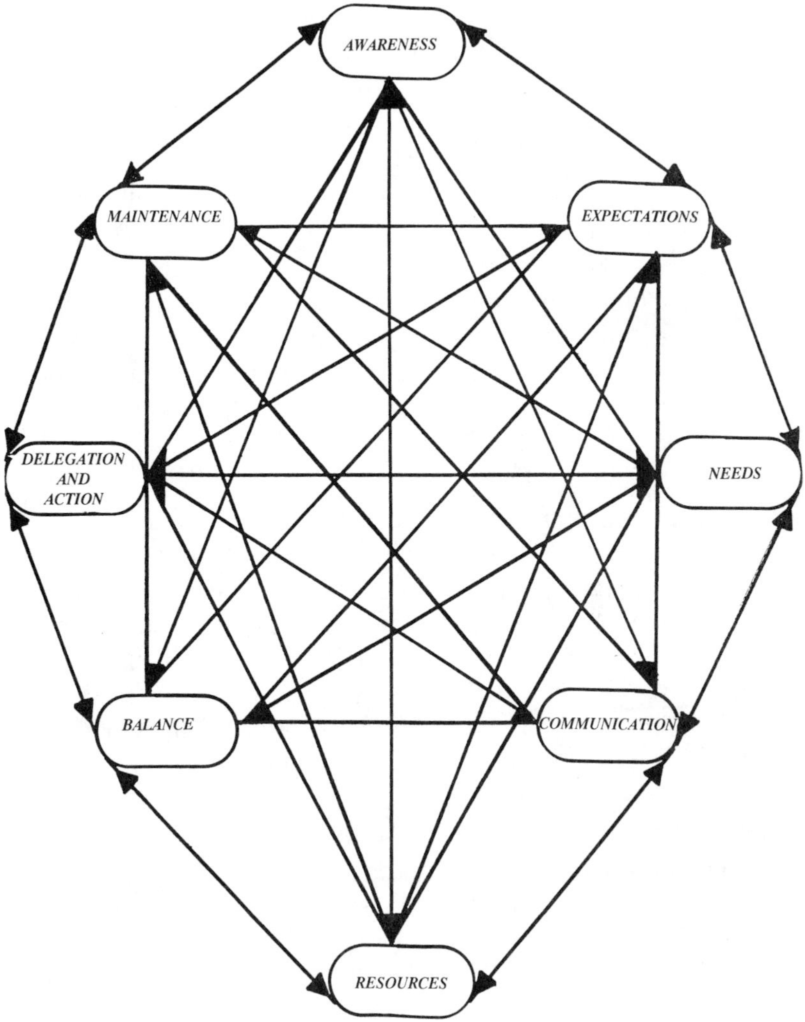

For example, you may find that you are actually in the middle—rather than at the beginning—of the process; therefore, it may make more sense for you to start with step three, *Needs,* because you already have a good grip on what everyone's *Expectations* (step two) are. Or you may find that between many of the steps you need to loop back to step one, *Awareness,* to remind yourself of the powerful emotions your mother's illness keeps raising in you. Or you may find that, although the process worked perfectly in the order described when you were caring for your father, now that you are caring for your aunt—who is much less demanding, but much more debilitated—you have to approach the situation in a different manner.

It's a flexible, elastic process, and it's meant to be used in whatever manner helps you the most. For example, there are exercises that go along with each step—if they are helpful, complete them; if they are not, pass them by, or perhaps just read through them. As you go along, mix it up, loop it back, vary it, adapt it. Make it work for you. The method is meant to be bent and stretched.

It is important to remember that what worked for your friend Leslie may not be what works best for you; she and her father may have personalities that compliment each other and allow them to live together easily--this may not be the case with you and your mother-in-law. You may find that what worked best when your father-in-law lost his vision is not as helpful now that your mother is depressed and lonely. This is why the method does not offer specific solutions; rather, it provides you with a means to determine, *for yourself,* what options and choices are best for you, in this particular situation, at this particular time.

You are caught in a constantly changing situation, and this is why you should expect to need to use The Balancing Act over and over again. For better or for worse, you are not confronting a one-shot crisis; the squeeze in which you are caught will last as long as you have some emotional responsibility for your parents, your children, your spouse, and yourself. Depending on the age, health, and number of your parents (or aunts or uncles or in-laws), and depending on the age, health, and number of your children, this period can last for decades.

The Balancing Act is comprised of eight steps that can be learned by reading this book and completing the exercises offered. Again, use the steps and the exercises as they are useful in your particular situation; if a specific exercise doesn't suit your style, or you just don't have enough time to do it, don't let it throw you, skim it for the concept and move on. The same holds true for the steps; skip them, reverse the order, go back to them—whatever works for you.

How ever you follow it, the method will still help you learn what you need to learn: how to sort out the complexities of your situation, separate everyone's real needs and expectations from their unrealistic and untenable ones, discover where communication patterns are stalled and how they can be improved, find available resources, and, finally, learn how to achieve some balance in your life—how to let go and share responsibility where it is possible and appropriate.

Again, just as your problems do not follow a straight, predictable line, neither does The Balancing Act. The method is not a march, it is a dance; the eight steps do not progress neatly and directly—although the book presents it that way to make the process easier to understand—the steps bob and weave and loop forward and back as needed by the specific and changing demands of your particular situation. As you can see from the figure on Page 17, there is no absolute end or beginning of the process; you will continually find yourself looping backward and forward through the steps to find what is most helpful for you in dealing with a particular problem at a particular time.

The Balancing Act is about acceptance—acceptance that aging and death are realities of life, acceptance that not all problems are able to be fixed or are under someone's control, acceptance that there are no perfect solutions, only choices between better and worse options. The method is about reasonable personal responsibility for everyone—for you, your spouse, your parents, and your children. It is about making your extended family system work—not work perfectly, just work as best it can. It is about distinguishing among everyone's wishes, hopes, expectations, and needs; it is about doing what you can about what you can—and about accepting that you cannot control the uncontrollable.

The Balancing Act is also about understanding and setting limits: on yourself and on what others can expect of you—setting limits without guilt. It is about getting over the need to control, and about sharing control with your parents, your siblings, your spouse, and your children; it is about letting go of things that don't work, about negotiating, sharing, and participating.

The Balancing Act is really about managing the stress of living life in the middle. It is about caring for yourself midstream in the life cycle, with parents at their stage, and children at their stage. It is about helping you handle it when everyone's stages seem out of synch and they all seem to be coming down on your head. It is about helping you and your family make the best choices possible, and finding a balance of responsibility among all of the players, with a maximum of communication and respect.

The Balancing Act will most likely show you that you and your family can find your balance by yourselves, but it also might show you that you and your family could benefit from discussing your problems with a professional—be it a physician, social worker, gerontologist, psychologist, or psychiatrist. For, while The Balancing Act *is* about the specific problems faced by the people in this situation, it may not be about the extreme problems some of you will face. The Balancing Act *will* help you deal with difficult family relationships, with elderly parents who may be ill, and with children who may be giving you a run for your money. But it is unfortunately beyond the scope of this book to delve deeply into the highly-specific problems of exceptionally dysfunctional families, or extremely demented parents, or violent teenagers. For these, you may need to seek additional help from professionals knowledgeable about your particular complications. But even in these extreme situations, The Balancing Act a good place to start. The following chart simplifies The Balancing Act.

The Balancing Act: Eight Steps to Equilibrium

STEP	RESULT
1) Awareness →→→→→	Figuring out who all the players are, and how they got involved. What really makes your family tick, and all the emotional issues raised by the revelation; plus how they affect your behavior.
2) Expectations →→→→	Recognizing expectations—yours and theirs, overt and covert, real, imagined, and misinterpreted.
3) Needs →→→→→→→	Differentiating needs from wishes, desires, and expectations—yours and theirs, overt and covert.
4) Communication→→→	Understanding your communication patterns—separating the covert and overt messages to improve communication.
5) Resources →→→→→	Discovering all the resources you and your family really have: people, services, community and government agencies.
6) Balance →→→→→→	Accepting the reality that you cannot do it all, letting go of the past, forgiving and accepting your parents and yourself—so you can select, prioritize, and start to make choices.
7) Delegation and Action→	Making choices, sharing, and problem-solving: a family get-together, delegation of responsibility, letting go.
8) Maintenance →→→→	Learning to use the method so it's available whenever you need it.

With this chart you can see the eight steps that make up The Balancing Act, plus a summary of each step and the intended result. Again, although at first glance the diagram may appear to present the method as a straight and linear process, it is not; the circular, interconnected figure on Page 17 is the way you should visualize The Balancing Act.

Step 1: Awareness

Awareness is the most complex step in The Balancing Act, and it is also one of the most crucial. This step incorporates awareness of many of the issues creating and affecting your uniquely personal situation:

1) Awareness of all the players involved--parents, children, spouses, extended family, in-laws, stepfamilies, co-workers, friends, neighbors— including who you think they are, who they really are, and the history behind how they got to be that way;
2) Awareness of relevant facts--aging, adolescence, child-rearing, finances, the finiteness of time and energy, the superwoman(man) syndrome—and knowledge and acceptance of these less-than-perfect realities;
3) Awareness of the complex emotional and psychological issues: fear of loss and death, repaying the parental debt, messages your behavior sends to your children, mid-life issues, needing to be needed, failure to meet expectations, desire to control the uncontrollable;
4) Self-awareness.

Acknowledging these issues and beginning to grapple with your feelings about them will help you begin to build a more realistic picture of your situation. This will help you understand many of the underlying emotions that affect everyone's behavior, and lay the groundwork for finding your balance.

Step 2: Expectations

The purpose of this step is to clarify the expectations held by all the important people involved in your Big Squeeze. It is imperative to look at not only your own expectations, but everyone else's, to try to figure out who is expecting what from whom and whether these expectations have any base in reality.

Many problems are rooted in the miscommunication of expectations. Often, an adult child puts herself out to do what she thinks her parent expects, when in reality the parent not only does not expect it, but does not want it. This step will help you understand why it is so difficult to be clear, and why people often send indirect signals rather than saying what they really mean. Understanding these issues, as well as your own overt and covert expectations, will help you discover the real expectations and accurately assess your ability and desire to meet them.

In trying to understand your own unrealistic expectations —perhaps to be a perfect daughter or son—you may need to loop back to step one and think about your feelings of having to *repay* your parents, and how these feelings might have been partially responsible for your untenable self-expectation.

Step 3: Needs

Differentiating between needs and desires—your parents', your children's, your spouse's, your boss', your friends', and your own—is tough, but crucial. This step helps you separate what he really needs from,

1) What he says he needs;
2) What he appears to need;
3) What you think he needs;
4) What you wish he needed.

Telling the difference between wishes, hopes, expectations, and needs is one of the ongoing processes that weave through all the steps of The Balancing Act. It's very hard to do, because the lines that separate the groups are often fuzzy, but it can be done.

For example, your feelings about your height and the aging process might be reflected in the following quotes: "I've always *wished* I were a few inches taller," "I *hope* I don't shrink too much as I age," "My mother and aunts suffered from osteoporosis, and I *expect* I will also have a problem with it," and "I *need* to talk to a doctor about taking calcium pills to try and combat the disease." As you can see, there is often little that can be done about wishes and hopes—except to recognize them for what they are, and to be aware of how they may affect your feelings and behavior—but expectations and needs tend to call for choice and action.

And what about your own needs? Are you always last? Do you recognize that you also have needs? Does anyone else—your parent, spouse, children, boss—recognize that your needs are part of the picture? What does this represent in terms of who you are?

This step should help you recognize that caring for yourself enables you to care for others. And perhaps a loop back to the sections on awareness and expectations will help you understand how you got into this situation, and what options you have for changing it.

Step 4: Communication

Clear communication patterns are another key to surviving the Big Squeeze. This step will help you see how communication can get muddled when messages are sent and mistakenly assumed to be correctly received.

Are there good or poor communication patterns within your family? A loop back to any, or all, of the first three steps may be useful at this point: What have you communicated to other family members about your needs or expectations? What have they heard? How have they communicated their needs or expectations to you? What have you heard? How do they all match?

This step will help you identify your own hidden and unclear messages, and discover hidden messages in the communications of others. Who is communicating what, and to whom? What is said versus what is really meant—and how you can tell the difference.

Step 5: Resources

Before you can assess the resources available to help you and your family, you must stop seeing yourself as the solution to the problem; in all likelihood you are both a piece of the solution *and* a piece of the problem. The fact that you are reading this book says a lot about your level and sense of responsibility; being the *responsible* one is a tough act. How did you become responsible for your parent? How do your parents feel about this? How about your siblings? Where are your siblings? How do you feel about this? Why you? Why now?

Your next move is to figure out what else is out there. There are many avenues of support available—from family members (including the elderly parent or young child who you assume is in need of support), to friendship networks, to local social service agencies, to state and federal subsidy programs. This step will help you discover and assess the support options that might be useful for you.

Step 6: Balance

It is almost impossible to find your balance point without accepting limitations—your own as well as those of the people and circumstances involved in your situation. This step will help you concede the difficult reality of being a "good enough" child with "good enough" parents, accept the past, and let go of the anger. Once you have come to grips with, and accepted, these truths and limitations, you will be able to make the choices you need to make—and come up with a plan to carry them out.

Step 7: Delegation and Action

In all likelihood the decisions and choices you need to make—and the ways you need to carry them out—will involve a sharing and delegation among all of the people in your situation. A loop back to step five might be useful to remind you of your resources, or maybe a loop to step six will bolster your ability to accept limitations.

Now you are ready to start to take the actions that will allow to you get some balance in your life. Others can take on more than you—or they—think. Your parent is not your child. Your child is not a helpless baby. Together, act on what you have learned.

Choice is the key. You need to be aware—as do all the others involved—that what you each perceive as a necessity is not necessarily that; what you perceive as a necessity is most likely a choice. Just because you feel you must have a spotless house does not mean that your mother—or your son, or your husband—feels the same. You choose to clean your mother's apartment. You choose to yell at your son for his messy room. You choose to feel guilt or anger, and, most likely, so does everyone else. You all need to recognize the element of choice in all your decisions, and how choice affects each person's reactions to the consequences of those decisions.

It is important to be aware that in some situations *action* can mean the choice to do nothing—for right now, or forever.

Sometimes action might be the internal process of telling yourself that it is not your choice to decide where your father will live, or it might be the decision to just let your mother live without a housekeeper because that is what *she* wants—regardless of whether it is what you would choose for her (or for yourself).

Other times, action might involve a family get-together: a calling together of all the affected people (be they just you and your parent, or all your siblings, in-laws and grandchildren, or you might wish to include an outside party such as a social worker or clergyperson) to help plan, problem-solve, and share responsibility. The goal of the get-together—and this step—is interdependence among all family members, with a true recognition and acceptance of everyone's capabilities and needs.

Step 8: Maintenance

Most likely, your Big Squeeze is going to go on for a long time. And most likely, it is going to change over that time: a parent will get sicker or healthier, your job will get more or less demanding, your children will grow, your marriage will become stronger, an in-law will die. It is because of this fact that The Balancing Act was designed to be flexible and adapt to each unique bend in your situation.

The danger of falling back into old patterns is always present, but it doesn't have to occur. Once you have mastered the first seven steps of the method, it is just a matter of jumping into the process wherever you need to, and using whatever piece you need at that time.

This final step will show you how to recognize the danger signs, and how to modify the method so that you can use it when you need it—for the present squeeze and for all the squeezes ahead of you.

Before the Balancing Act ...

Louise Broderick, a school nurse with three teen-age children, was furious with her sister Natalie, her brother Joe, and her parents. *She* was the only one who would accept the reality of the inevitable. *She* was the only one who would admit that their parents—both in their eighties—were in failing health. It was the way it had always been: *she* was the one Mom called when there was trouble, *she* was the one who ran to their aid in the middle of the night, *she* was the one who took responsibility for solving the problem—particularly if it was medical.

Once again, *she* was the one who was scouring newspapers, looking into apartments, elderly housing, retirement homes, and homemakers. And now that she had finally found a wonderful and convenient nursing home for her parents, no one—her parents included—wanted any part of it. *They* all said to leave well enough alone. *They* all said she was—as always—trying to fix a problem nobody had.

* * * *

Donald Moran, a divorced college professor with a 20-year-old son, lived in a small house around the corner from his parents. When his father died, Donald supported his mother in every way he could. But he soon realized that his mother—a very dependent woman in the best of times—felt unable to make a move without him: she couldn't fill her car with gas, or go shopping in town, or deal with estate issues unless Donald was involved. His own life was completely revolving around her needs; one day Donald realized that he was becoming his father.

... And After the Balancing Act

"We know there might be problems, but we'd rather deal with them than lose our independence," Louise's mother said at their family get-together. Natalie and Joe convinced Louise that, although she had the right to offer options to her parents, they had the right to make their own decisions; Louise reluctantly canceled the retirement-home plans.

A week after this family decision, Louise's mother called to say that her father had had some difficulty breathing and, although he seemed fine now, Louise should come right over. Louise asked for a few details, and told her mother that she didn't think it sounded bad enough to warrant the hour drive. She told her mother to call the doctor in the morning, and 911 if there was any reoccurrence before then.

Louise didn't sleep much that night. She lay awake reminding herself that her parents had chosen to stay in their own home and accept the consequences. She reminded herself that although she couldn't control their choices, she could—and was—controlling her responsibility for their choices. Finally she slept.

Louise called her mother as soon as she got up. Her parents had just come back from their morning walk, and her father was feeling so well that he decided he didn't need to call the doctor after all—another choice Louise disagreed with, but nevertheless a choice she had to accept.

* * * *

Donald realized that taking on his father's role was detrimental to both himself and his mother. So he and his mother sat down, talked about it, and came up with an *independence plan.* Instead of filling up her car himself, Donald went with his mother to the gas station while she had it filled; then the next month she did it by herself. When Mrs. Moran had a question about her homeowner's policy, and Donald reminded her that she could get the phone number from the policy and call the insurance agent herself, she balked but finally called. The day her kitchen drain got clogged she didn't bother Donald at school; she just called the plumber. Donald thought his mother's friend Muriel might make a nice roommate and help share expenses. Mrs. Moran rejected the idea and Donald dropped it.

Donald still comes to dinner almost every night, but last Friday Mrs. Moran had to cancel because she was serving at the church supper. At first Donald felt a little sad that his mother was too busy for him, but then he called his friend Mark and they met for dinner in town.

Intergenerational Issues

Caught In The Web

Gail Clark stared into the depths of her coffee cup, but the dark liquid gave her no answers. Minna had been her mother-in-law for fifteen years; they had hit it off the first time John introduced them, and had been extremely close throughout her marriage—even during the more distressing stages of the divorce. In the last year the poor woman had lost both her husband and her daughter, and neither of her sons had been able to give her much support: John's energy was drained by his own grief and the responsibilities of his expanding business; Joe lived 2,000 miles away.

Minna had spiraled downward into a depression that left her almost immobile, and Gail had been horrified when she stopped by unexpectedly and discovered her ex-mother-in-law hollow-eyed and dehydrated amidst the squalor of an apartment that hadn't been cleaned for a month. She immediately began calling doctors, cleaning, and almost force-feeding the older woman.

At first her husband, Ken, had been completely behind her attempts to help Minna, but lately he had become less supportive, citing the extraordinary demands of their life: new home, new marriage, four children all recently rattled by the divorce and remarriage of their parents, his ailing grandfather, his job, her community responsibilities.

Ken said that if things were different he would have no qualms about her spending so much time with Minna, but that, given the circumstances, her first priority had to be to her current family. Gail agreed in theory, but if she didn't drive Minna to the doctor, arrange for the correct medications with the pharmacist, and make sure there was enough food in the refrigerator, who would?

Gail is caught—caught in the complex web of multiple-family relationships. And she should probably prepare herself for the strands to get more numerous, more interwoven, and more demanding; for she is surrounded by three immediate families: her family of birth, her family of her first marriage, and her family of her second marriage. A genogram of Gail's family is shown below.

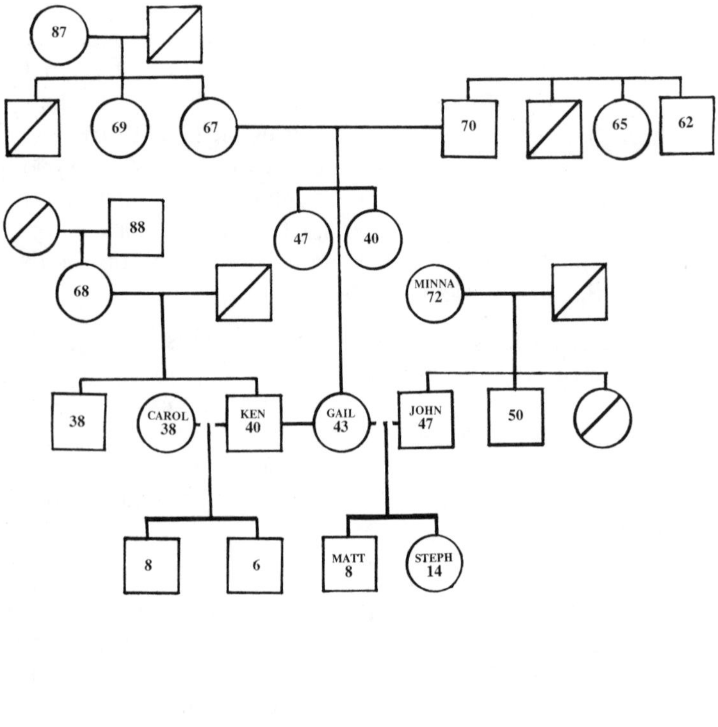

Gail's family circumstances are the proverbial double-edged sword. On one hand, she is surrounded by a multitude of supportive and positive relationships; she has love, friendship, companionship. On the other hand, each of these relationships carries with it the possibility of high demand—and some intense, deep-seated emotion.

Gail's immediate family includes five members from her family of birth (her parents, two sisters, and a grandmother), four from the family of her first marriage (her son, daughter, ex-husband, and ex-mother-in-law) and five from the family of her second marriage (her husband, his two sons, his mother, and his grandfather). And this doesn't include aunts or uncles, or her second husband's in-laws, aunts, or uncles—or his ex-wife.

Of her immediate fourteen relationships, six relatives are over the age of 65 and four are under 21. It's no wonder Gail is in distress; she's a woman in the middle, a woman caught in the web. Your situation, although different in its particulars, is probably similar to Gail Clark's in terms of the complexity and interconnectedness of your personal networks.

No Family Is An Island

It has been said that no (wo)man is an island, and this is also true of families. Each family is part of a *greater whole* that includes all the people and organizations with which each family member is associated. Looking back at Gail Clark's genogram, a partial listing of her *greater whole* can be made.

Gail is an active member of her community and is currently on the volunteer staff of the town library. Through her church, she tutors under-privileged children and she is on the Board of Directors of the Teen Hotline. After living in town for twenty years, she has a wide group of friends and acquaintances, and enjoys an active social life.

Each one of these groups and activities is part of Gail's *greater whole.* Each one can be the source of satisfaction and pleasure—and each one can also be the source of pressure and demand.

But Gail's *greater whole* doesn't stop with her own involvements; Gail is touched and affected by the networks and concerns of every other member of her immediate family. Her son, Matthew, has been having a difficult time with the divorce. He has been withdrawn and hostile, and his school work has suffered; just last week Gail met with his third-grade teacher to discuss the problem. Her daughter, Stephanie, is a freshman in high school; a quiet girl, she spends most of her time ice skating. She came in third in a regional figure-skating competition last year, and her love of the sport often has her—and Gail—at the local ice-skating rink at 5:00 a.m.

And then there's John's business, in which Gail still retains partial ownership. And Minna's doctor's appointments. And Ken's divorce, which was much less amiable than hers and has generated a series of ongoing problems that have become a part of her everyday life. And Ken's two sons, whose weekend visits are full of hostility, as well as chauffeuring duties to soccer, T-ball, and gymnastics. And Ken's mother, who needs support with her father's recent forgetfulness and the final liquidation of her late husband's business. And the double whammy of two sets of holidays and family obligations generated by Ken's synagogue and Gail's church. And then there's ....

And then there's her mother and father who are always ready to lend a hand, be it taking Matthew on an outing or helping Ken install storm windows. And her sister, married to a successful businessman, who set up college trust funds for Stephanie and Matthew. And her new neighbors who took in the mail while Gail and Ken were on their honeymoon and waited for the washing machine repairman the morning of Minna doctor's appointment. And her friend Linda, who as her divorce lawyer had worked with John's lawyer to make a painful experience as painless as possible. And Ralph, the second-grade boy she tutored last year who told her how he had survived his parent's divorce and found that he was actually happier now that they weren't together. And there's ....

The Ripple Effect

State and local cuts had devastated the Teen Hotline's budget and each board member was asked to cover the phones one evening a week until fund-raising activities produced more revenue. Gail didn't have the time but couldn't refuse, knowing the extraordinary need.

Ken was supportive, and made dinner and oversaw homework every Tuesday night while she sat in the high-school basement counseling troubled teenagers. Everything held together until one evening when Ken was home alone with Matthew and his ex-wife, Carol, called. She was hysterical: a pipe had burst in the house, water was running through two floors and into the basement, and she couldn't find the shut-off valve. Ken had to come immediately.

Ken had just put Matthew to bed and he was loathe to wake the child; they had had their first really decent evening together—miraculously free of whining for Mom or bedtime power plays—and Ken didn't want to spoil the effect.

He called Gail, but she couldn't abandon the phones; he tried John, but got his answering machine. Finally, after a being reduced to begging, he talked his mother into coming over. She had to bring his grandfather—who was especially confused that evening—and she made it plain that she was annoyed with both Ken and Gail for the inconvenience.

Ken raced to Carol's and arrived just as the fire department was leaving; they had found the shut-off valve in the back corner of the flooded basement. Carol was furious with him for taking so long.

When Gail finally got home Ken was frustrated and angry. He told her she had to stop working at the Hotline. She refused and they had the first—but far from the last—major argument of their marriage.

* * * *

It's a system—an interconnected, interwoven, interdependent system. A push, a change, a demand in one place has the potential to affect all the others. Things as seemingly insignificant as a temporary favor for a community agency, or the breakdown of a household appliance, can wreak havoc in an overcommitted life.

And it never ends. In a life as rich and as complex as Gail's there will always be demands and commitments pulling in more directions than a human being can possibly go, requiring more hours than there are in a day, and ultimately, forcing a person without survival skills to feel frustrated, incompetent, and guilty.

The key is to develop the survival skills. To become aware of all the people and pressures that simultaneously impinge on your life. To learn to delegate without guilt, to set limits, to say "no" when you need to. To separate the things that can be done from the things that can't be done. To accept that you can't control and fix everything—and to accept the feelings that come with facing the fact that you can't do it all.

Where Are You, And Where Are They?

Where Are You?

Catherine Gant paused before the door; her heart was pounding and her fingers were trembling. Was this the right thing to do? She looked into the room; it was filling up with students—with their clear eyes, smooth cheeks, and slender body lines that cried "youth." Catherine stepped back into the corridor. This was absurd. What was she doing with these children? She felt much closer in age and place to her mother-in-law's bridge club than she did to these college kids whose life she was going to be sharing.

She stepped forward again. Yes, it was the right thing. It was time that she took control, time for her to be the driver instead of being driven by the needs of everyone else—driven by the role she had once so heartily embraced. She had half her life before her; she was going to do what she really wanted to do. Her kids had agreed to share dinner duties and do their own laundry. Jim was going to take over the dusting and vacuuming. His sister was going to take Mother Rose to her weekly physical therapy sessions.

Catherine took a deep breath and walked into the classroom. She sat down at the nearest desk and faced the blackboard. She pulled out her brand-new notebook and pen. She was finally going to get a college degree.

* * * *

Jeff Tuite looked around the conference room; it was full of men in dark suits and red ties, and women in dark suits and silk blouses. He glanced down at his own navy pin–striped jacket; he loosened the maroon tie that was cutting into his windpipe. Was this really what he wanted to be doing with his life? His wife and two kids were packing for their trip to Florida to visit both sets of grandparents. He was staying home to battle for the development of a software system that would be obsolete a year after it was installed—and to clearly establish his place over the two young Harvard MBAs nipping at his corporate heels.

Jeff glanced over at his boss, an overworked, overextended divorced woman who looked ten years older than her age. Suddenly it hit him—he didn't want her job. Let the B-school kids have it. After half a lifetime spent climbing a corporate ladder that led nowhere, he didn't want to waste the rest. He wanted more time with his family; he would go to Miami with them! Maybe his in-laws would even take the kids for a day or two and he and Roxanne could escape for some much-needed time alone. He wanted to spend more time with his father before the cancer made the elderly man too weak. And his mother—the mother who had seen him through all his tough times—now needed support.

Jeff rose to give his presentation. He made eye contact with each person at the table, and he smiled. There was bound to be opposition, but he would find a way. After all, the life he had remaining was all that he had; he was going to do with it what he wished.

* * * *

Lisa Kramer stared at the flickering TV set. Oprah was earnestly discussing teenage suicide with some *attempt-survivors.* Although teenage suicide was far from Lisa's problem, something about the issue intrigued her; she felt a strange sense of recognition, of identification, with the troubled kids. Then it clicked. She related because she *did* feel like a disjointed teenager: the same turmoil, the same restlessness and free-floating anger, the same questions about the real meaning of life and death and the futility of it all. But she was far from her teenage years; her hips were widening, her back aching, and, rather than standing at the threshold of adulthood, her life was half gone.

She picked up the remote and Oprah disappeared with the touch of a button. Lisa stared at the silent, blank screen.

* * * *

So, where are you? Most likely you are *in the middle,* just like Catherine, Jeff, and Lisa. Being in the middle means that when you look behind and ahead you see roughly equivalent lengths of time—when you start to think in terms of years left, rather than in years since you were born. It also means that you begin to reexamine and reevaluate how you spent the first half of your life, and make plans for how you want to spend the second.

Life in the middle

Some experts in the field of adult development say that life in the middle is much like adolescence—that it has the same turmoils, the same search for identity, the same struggle to come to grips with an incomprehensible world. Others say that life in the middle is worse than adolescence—that in addition to adolescent-like traumas, the mid-life person must face loss of youth, come to grips with mortality, and accept that there are no absolute answers. Still others say that mid-life is qualitatively different from any other stage.

What the experts *do* agree on is this: in almost all instances, life in the middle is a time of crisis, particularly for those whose lives have not measured up to their expectations (due to divorce, difficulties with children and/or parents, stagnating careers, or downward mobility). Yet, while this crisis may bring pain, it also brings opportunity for those who are able to learn from their mistakes and are capable of adjustment; for, on the other side, lies self-discovery and growth.

Adult development

Human development does not stop with adulthood, as the reams of books and articles on child development would often lead one to believe. Human life is motion, perpetual movement; it's a constant reaction to, and action upon ongoing events. Human beings are always in the process of adapting and changing—reaching a new phase, dealing with its issues and problems, and emerging on the other side, hopefully wiser and better able to face the issues and problems of the next phase.

And, just as each individual has a unique face—even though all human faces are comprised of two eyes, a single nose, and a mouth—so too, each individual has a unique life experience—even though all human lives are comprised of a similar set of developmental phases.

Erik Erickson says that there are eight ages of man: eight stages through which each one of us must pass from birth to old age, each with its own particular crisis to be solved.[1] If we solve it, we move on; if we do not, we carry it with us into the next stage. Developmental change, according to Erickson, is the result of combined biological, psychological, and social forces, and that each demand and conflict has its own time. Although the specifics of his theories have been disputed (eight stages, or twelve, or perhaps twenty? biology over psychology? beyond the eighth stage?), when it comes to the big picture, Erickson is right: from the first day to the last, the human organism is constantly adjusting, and changing, and growing.

1. Erikson, Erik. *Childhood and Society.* New York: Norton, 1950.

Developmental issues of life in the middle

So what are your issues? What are the crises and problems and dilemmas with which you must deal because you are in the middle of your life?

The half-way mark ("the apostrophe in time between the end of growing up and the beginning of growing old," as Gail Sheehy puts it) seems to bring about an increased sensitivity to the realities of life and time: I am mortal and so is everything I value; the world is in flux and so am I.[2] It also brings about a heightened awareness of one's place in the world: who am I? is this who I want to be?

When taken together, these feelings and questions lead to an assessment—a stock-taking—of life: where am I going and how do I get there? These questions are made more urgent by the underlying knowledge that if action is not taken now, it may never be, and the fear that the years will slide into a monotonous sameness.

So you are thrown off balance. There is a need—almost a drive—to change. You look around. You see that your stomach is not as flat as it used to be, that the old woman coming toward you is your mother, that the almost-adult woman in the restaurant is your daughter; you see that nothing is forever. You feel closer in time, wisdom, and judgement to your father than to your son, and you begin to wonder if the person you always thought you were, might not be who you are; neither the jeans nor the roles quite fit anymore. And you realize that perhaps it's not such a bad thing.

You seek to discover your own life. To separate the dreams from the reality, to accept who you are, and to define the parameters of who you can become. To determine what the future should look like and how to make it truly yours—not just the reflection of the way someone told you it should be. To get control of your direction, your destination, and your

2. Sheehy, Gail. *Passages.* New York: Dutton, 1976.

mode of transportation. And then, perhaps, to look beyond yourself—to reach out to the world, to the younger generation, to help them in their journey through life.

What am I doing? Why am I here? Is this all there is? What do I really believe in? Who do I want to be? Am I capable? Can I make it happen? Time isn't forever.

Male and female differences. Although the underlying sensitivities and questions are the same, men's and women's mid-life issues are slightly different, most likely because of differences in roles and expectations. Interestingly, the end result is a blurring of some of the standard sex-typed priorities and behaviors (women as passive and family-oriented, men as aggressive and career-oriented).

The typical mid-life woman begins her reexamination earlier than the typical man. When a woman decides she isn't going to have any more children (often around 35) she is freed up, her energy peaks, and her quest for the next phase of her life is actively pursued. When a man begins to feel threatened by the young "whippersnappers" entering the profession he has dedicated himself to for 20 or 25 years (usually a bit after 40), he slows down and asks himself what is truly important in life. She becomes more aggressive and independent, and seeks her place in the *real world*; he tends toward increased introspection, more involvement with his family, and a mentorship role in his work.

What is occurring is, in actuality, the same for both sexes: a striving for unique individuality, a capturing of the piece that was missing in the first half of life. These issues manifest themselves in seemingly opposite behavior because, almost by definition, traditional sex roles are exclusionary. Mid-life allows a choosing, a melding; it allows an individual to decide which pieces to discard, which to keep, and which to take up.

The mid-life couple. Although the underlying developmental issues may be the same for both sexes—and the end result is increased similarity—the process for a couple working through their mid-life issues can be very difficult indeed.

She is pushing herself outward, he is reaching inward; she is seeking to aggressively expand beyond the family, he is seeking to reconnect with it; she may be feeling self-confident and powerful, he is not quite so sure of himself. Although working from the same issues and striving for the same individual ends, they are often at odds.

Each is questioning and striving and adapting, dealing with his or her own issues. When she turns to him, she may find an irritable, self-absorbed person, a person she barely recognizes. When he reaches out to her, instead of the support he had always known, he may find a wife who is withdrawing herself at a time when he craves unconditional love. Anxiety, uncertainty, and anger are common, often accompanied by communication failures and disturbances of intimacy. It is not surprising that rates of marital dissatisfaction rise at this stage of life.

But the news is not all bad. For those who successfully stay together through mid-life, marital satisfaction is high; a mellowing, an increased confidence in self, spouse, and marriage often occurs. The successful post-mid-life couple seem to recognize, and accept, the futility of trying to completely understand each other or the world. They start to let go of illusions, of children, of unimportant trappings. Their privacy and their friends gain in importance, satisfaction with both marriage and life increase.

So, now you know where you are, but ...

Where Are They?

Artie stood uncertainly in the doorway as Marjorie and her mother raged at each other. "I'm 21 years old and I'll go with him if I want to!" Marjorie screamed.

"You're not going anywhere, young lady! This is my house and as long as you're under my roof you will do as I say! And I say you may not run out with this boy at eleven o'clock at night and go off to God-knows-where for God-knows-how-long!"

"I'm going! I did it when I was at college and I'll do it now." Marjorie pulled her coat from the closet, grabbed Artie by the arm and ran out the door.

* * * *

"Me do it!" 2-year-old Malcolm exclaimed, pulling his sneaker from his father's hand. "Me do it!"

Robert Hajjar gently pried the shoe from the tightly-coiled little fingers. "Not this morning, Mal. I'm late for work," he said calmly.

"Me! Me! Mal! Me!"

"Not this morning," Robert repeated, his voice becoming more stern as he tried to push Malcolm's foot into the sneaker.

Malcolm yanked his foot from his father's hand and threw himself down on the kitchen floor, pounding it with his fists. "No! No! No! Me do it! Me do it!"

Unable to get either kicking foot anywhere near a sneaker, Robert finally picked up Malcolm and threw him in the car without his shoes. The child was still screaming, and Robert knew he was going to be even later for work.

* * * *

"But Mother Davis, you know that on Monday's you go to the Senior Center. You know I tutor on Monday," Gerri Davis pleaded with her mother-in-law. "You know you can't stay here alone."

"I stayed alone fine when I was in my own apartment in Deerfield."

"You know you couldn't stay there after Dad died—you know it was too far for Dave or me to drive. You had to move here." Gerri tried in vain to get the older woman out of her chair.

"So you say."

"Your friend Mrs. Mitchell is there on Mondays ..."

The older woman sighed. "I may have to get used to my knees not quite working right, that your father-in-law's gone, that there are things that can never be ... but *I don't* like Mrs. Mitchell, and *I don't* like the Senior Center, and *I don't* have to go." She smiled sweetly. "So I'm going to stay right here."

* * * *

Where are they? They are in the middle of their own developmental crises, riding the waves—and dropping in the troughs—of their own life cycle. They are battling, and adapting, and changing to the rhythms of their own phases—and sometimes they are battling you.

But if you are aware of where they are—what their concerns are, what and why they are fighting—it will be easier for you to forestall the battles, reduce your stress, and ultimately survive your Big Squeeze.

Infancy and early childhood

This stage of life contains so much growth and change it is almost incomprehensible: learning to walk, to talk, to eat, to eliminate, to hold a crayon, to share toys, to differentiate the inside from the outside, and, perhaps most importantly, learning when to hold on and when to let go. The life-long journey of self-discovery begins: I am a separate, unique human person—but, who am I?

The baby discovers that if she lets that loud noise rise from her throat, someone will feed her; she holds a hand in front of her face and recognizes it as uniquely her own; she looks in the mirror and understands that the smile reflected there belongs only to her. The child grasps he is different, separate, unique—he is not his brother, or mother, or father—and he says "no" to try and discover who that different and separate and unique being might be.

Middle childhood

This stage is all about melding a growing self-image with the skills and tools a child needs to achieve adulthood. Erikson speaks of a spirit "tamed and harnessed by school," others see a more gentle tutorage and shaping, and yet others describe a period of head-butting and bloody battles that results in the preliminary form of a socialized being.[3]

The child learns how to play soccer and comfort her little brother when he cries. He learns how to read newspaper headlines, write to Grandma, and how to make change at his lemonade stand. She learns there are bad guys and good guys, and how to tell the difference. When a friend comes over to visit, the bedroom door is securely closed. On Halloween, they dress up like evil witches, and collect money to buy medicine for poor children. They are often obedient and good-natured at school, not so obedient and good-natured at home.

Adolescence

Puberty strikes and the child becomes unraveled; he who was before is no more. In his place is an unrecognizable person, a disorganized mess of hormones, and restlessness and discontent; he looks different, he acts different, he *is* different. But he does not know yet who he is. By definition, adolescence is a time when she must let go of the past, for she cannot discover who she *is* until she loosens the bonds of who she *was*. And often—much to most parents' chagrin—this discovery comes through explorations into who she is not.

3. Erikson, Erik. *Childhood and Society.* New York: Norton, 1950.

He falls blindly in love with a girl with whom he has nothing in common—or worse, with one whose interest he can never attain. She is only concerned with how she is perceived by a crowd whose taste leaves much to be desired; the sweet child who befriended the girl with cerebral palsy, now wouldn't be caught dead speaking to someone wearing jeans without the correct designer label. Parents know nothing; teenagers know all. They are fighting to be different—from their parents as well as all other adults. They are searching for a new independence, a true definition of self.

And yet, they are not quite willing to let go of childhood: her shelves are still filled with Barbie dolls and he still sleeps with "Dunkin," the stuffed dinosaur of his toddler days—although now he is very careful to hide the toy under his pillow. When she isn't invited to *the* party of the year, she climbs into her mother's lap and cries like a baby. When he gets punched in the eye by the neighborhood bully, he turns to his father for boxing lessons. The next day she's contrary and argumentative; he declares he's going to join the marines.

Young adulthood

The jig's up: she has graduated from college, can drink, vote, and sign contracts—adulthood has arrived and childhood is over. The problem is that she still isn't sure what she wants, she still isn't sure who she is. There's so much to decide: the Peace Corp or law school? San Francisco or Boston? Marc or Andrew, or no one until she's 30? Perhaps she'd better live at home for a while? Or maybe on a kibbutz?

He is simultaneously drawn and repelled at the idea of entering the family business; working with the father he idolizes, coming home to a beautiful wife, perhaps a couple of kids—but not quite now, maybe later, when he's grown up. She's never going to have a family, a career is the only way for her—until she sees her cousin Rachel's baby and thinks, "Well, maybe someday, when I'm grown up."

They are there and they are not there; caught between the desire to finally grow up and become defined, and the need to scout it all out for just a little bit longer.

Mid-life

And then there's you—smack dab in the middle of it all. You are working on finding yourself a niche—establishing yourself in your family, your job, your community. You are in the stage of maximum productivity, but also maximum interdependence; both those older and those younger look to you for love and support.

Toward the end of this stage you may find that your children are beginning to leave the nest, your parents are visibly aging, your career has hit a plateau. Suddenly, you have time to think and reflect—and even some time for hobbies or leisure. Retirement beckons and you look towards it with both anticipation and fear. There is a new appreciation of the now—a time that seems better and more precious than either the past or the future—and a new appreciation of yourself.

Later maturity

When suddenly you are 5'3" instead of 5'4", when waitresses never enunciate their words clearly enough for you to catch the dinner specials, and when the face in the mirror contains more wrinkles than your grandmother's ever had, it's hard to view the future with lots of anticipation. Especially when the woman on the television is spreading wrinkle cream on a face that can't be more than 25. Especially when almost half of your high-school graduating class didn't show up for the fifty-fifth reunion because they had all passed away. Especially when your *baby* brother has just retired.

The young child is always in a hurry to get to the future, a future he perceives to be far better than the present. The mid-life person is generally content where she is, for her favorable or unfavorable view of the present is roughly equivalent to her feelings about the past and the future. But with older people it's not quite so simple, for a variety of factors—biological, sociological, psychological, and situational—affect an individual's evaluation of his or her place in time.

A woman with strong genes and good heath, adequate finances, a supportive family (often including a living spouse), the personality and intellectual power to review her life and find it acceptable—as well as a strong dose of good luck—should reach a maturity marked by serenity, wisdom, and relative happiness. On the other hand, a man whose luck has run in the opposite direction, who perceives his life as a failure, and who can't accept the advent of his own death, will find his present meaningless and depressing, far worse than the past. And unfortunately, no matter how an older individual views the present, due to the realities of growing old in a society that devalues aging, the future is always seen as a much less desirable place to be.

And in some ways this perception is not unrealistic; the final stages of life are full of losses—biological and sociological. The body is wearing down: skin wrinkles, bones stiffen, colors lose their richness, sounds become muted, the stomach and intestines just don't work the way they used to. Friends are dying, spouses, siblings, and cousins are frail and dependent—there are no more parents, uncles, or aunts. Children are independent and self-absorbed, the retirement party is far in the past, the young girl in the drug store treats you as if you were a child, and the nurse discusses your incontinence with the doctor as if you were not in the room. It's not easy growing old in America; Rodney Dangerfield would recognize the problem—you "don't get no respect."

Erickson says the developmental task of later maturity is striving for integrity,[4] Peck says it's ego transcendence,[5] and other theorists talk of interiority or disengagement or acceptance; but whatever the name, the underlying meaning is roughly the same: trying to get some respect, striving to maintain a sense of dignity based on your years of life experience—in defiance of the labels everyone seems to be trying to pin on you.

For if you believe society's message (the aging are *less* than the young), if you take what *they* say at face value and apply it to yourself, you have lost—and you will never get the respect due you. You will lose self esteem, and others will lose even more esteem for you. If you buy into this message, you will allow this distorted image to become a mirror, a looking-glass: what *they* say about you is true, because you aren't standing up and defying the reflection you see in their eyes.

But this need not be the case. For this stage of life is about that final reevaluation, the reassessment that is going to put it all together, that is going to give it some meaning, and make it make sense. And you have control over how this all comes out. If you can make a positive assessment—look back with satisfaction and ahead without fear, recognize that your contributions will survive beyond the life of your body, accept the realities of biology—then you will have achieved integrity and ego transcendence, and gotten yourself some respect.

But it isn't easy. It isn't easy to be the only animal cognizant of its own death. It isn't easy to grow old in a society that devalues aging. It isn't easy to experience loss after loss. And it is especially difficult to try and grapple with these issues when your main source of support—your family—is undergoing such rapid changes.

4. Erikson, Erik. *Childhood and Society.* New York: Norton, 1950.
5. Peck, Robert. "Psychological Developments in the Second Half of Life." Washington, DC: American Psychological Association, 1956.

Today's elderly grew up in the first half of the twentieth century; it would have been impossible for any of them to imagine the family at the dawn of the twenty-first: working women, first babies at 40, divorce, remarriage, reconstituted families, geographical dispersion. Nor could they have imagined the complex medical, social, and caretaking bureaucracies that have such a significant role in their lives. The elderly are facing the unfaceable, and grappling with the ungrapplable, amidst the chaotic sea of modern American life.

In many ways you are their anchor. And in many ways you are not. Your parents may look to you to hold them in place, to keep them from being swept away by the tides of time—but you can't always do that. For no matter how hard you try, and no matter how good a job you do, you don't have that much control—you can't keep them from growing old, you can only support them as they face the challenge.

When Cycles Intersect, But It's Out of Sync

"I'm too young to have to deal with this right now!" is the cry of the sandwich generation. And you are right: you are too young; you weren't brought up to expect to be dealing with aging parents while you still had dependent children, and had just barely begun to work out your own mid-life issues. You expected to *launch* your children, to have them out on their own, and to have completed your reassessment and reexamination before your parents started aging.

But now you find that you are the bridge. You are supporting and helping the younger generation reach its adulthood, while you are also supporting and helping the older generation find its way through old age. The younger generation stays around longer than it used to; young people are economically more dependent than you were at that age. The older generation is confused; there are few role models for positive aging, and the bureaucratic jungle of services and costs is difficult to travel alone. Everyone needs you. And they need you in ways you never anticipated.

It's off-time, out of sync—and that makes it all that much harder. You're already overloaded, you're not developmentally ready, you didn't expect it, you're not prepared—it just isn't the right time; but it's here. Blame it on modern medicine, blame it on the women's movement, blame it on the recession—blame whomever or whatever you want; but it's here and it's not going away.

You may feel anger and resentment, and perhaps a bit of shame for these emotions. Or you may be clothing yourself in a state of shock or denial that keeps you from feeling anything at all. Or maybe you are experiencing sadness, emptiness, and fear. Or perhaps you flip-flop among all of these.

Whatever you feel, chances are it's pretty normal; it's natural to feel you have been deceived. You've been tricked by your parents: you thought they would always be there to protect you, and they have broken their promise—they too are mortal, and their mortality points up your own. And you've been tricked by society: you were supposed to be much older when your parents got old.

It's okay to have all these feelings; you just can't let them motivate you to make the wrong choices. It's okay for emotions to motivate—love and caring are often powerful and positive motivators—you just have to be clear about what the emotions are, and how they affect your choices.

And when these feelings are inappropriate, you can't let them get in the way of the things that need to be faced or the actions that need to be taken. So kick and scream for a while if that's what you feel is necessary. Act like a spoiled member of the "me" generation, and get it out of your system. Then sit down and look at the situation. Sit down and face the facts.

But this isn't easy either. Because sometimes the facts are not the facts—sometimes the facts are not black and white, but are various and complex shades of gray. Sometimes facts are perceptions—yours, theirs, or society's. Sometimes facts are wrong. And, as if these gray facts were not hard enough to deal with, the situation is further complicated because in almost all cases there are *no absolute right* answers either.

So what can you do? You can ask the right questions. You can get all the relevant information. You can be aware of the complex system in which you live—and of all the emotional and practical issues of your particular family, in its particular life cycle, at this particular time. Then you will be able to figure out your options and be in a position to make the best choices.

SECTION II

The Balancing Act

STEP 1
Awareness

The Cast

"If only we had one more person," Kimberly Han complained to her friend Allysa as they sat in her bedroom. "One more person and we could play hearts—I hate honeymoon bridge." Allysa nodded and they frowned at each other. "I hate boring Saturday afternoons," Kimberly whined. "If only Megan could have come over ..."

It never occurred to Kimberly that her grandfather, who was reading the paper in the living room, could be their third hand for cards. And he would make a far better third than she could ever have imagined, for he was a devoted bridge player.

* * * *

Eleanor Osterman shook her head sadly. "We won't be able to go to Vermont with you," she told her friend Phyllis. "Andrew can't do the overnight—I wish he were more independent, but I don't feel right pushing him. Remember the Cub Scout's camp-out two summers ago? Remember Howard had to go up and get him in the middle of the night? There's no point in my even asking ..."

"Gee, that sounds awesome," Andrew Osterman said to his friend Seth. "A whole night in the woods!" Then his face fell.

"But my mom'll never let me. She thinks I'm still a baby. She'll just yack on and on about all that stuff that happened at Cub Scouts ages ago." He threw his hands in the air and slumped in his chair. "There's no point even asking ..."

* * * *

Two days before Thanksgiving, Sandy Koehler waited impatiently at the supermarket check-out counter. The line was long and she had 3000 things to do before the family—all 22 of them—arrived for dinner on Thursday. She used to love having Thanksgiving at her house—before she had two kids, before Dad moved in, before she had resumed her social-work career. Now she'd do anything to get someone else to have it at their house—Cindy or Natalie or Derek's sister Nina. But she knew it had become a family tradition to have Thanksgiving at her house, and no one else would ever offer.

Sandy didn't notice her sister-in-law, Nina, standing in front of the poultry section, staring longingly at a large turkey. Nina was wishing that *she* could have Thanksgiving dinner at her house. But she knew Sandy loved having the party, and would never relinquish control of such an important family event.

* * * *

The types of mistakes that Kimberly, Eleanor, and Sandy made are more common than you might think; and the results can be much more devastating than a missed card game or a forfeited trip to Vermont. Lack of awareness of who a person really is can have disastrous consequences. For example, if you make a decision to put your elderly father in a nursing home—based on an incorrect assessment that he can't take care of himself—his anger and bad behavior could lead to excessive sedation, and his frustration and unhappiness to an early death. If you erroneously assume your teenage son isn't capable of handling a part-time job, and deny him the opportunity, your label of *no confidence* could lead to lower self-esteem, negatively affecting many other areas of his life. Or, perhaps it's your mistaken ideas about yourself: your assumption that you are superwoman, and can do it all, could lead to physical and mental burn out, rendering you useless to everyone—including yourself.

The human mind creates categories in an attempt to organize and comprehend the world. While categorization is an extremely intelligent and useful way to handle information, it can also be very dangerous. The hazards are obvious when talking of racial or religious stereotypes, but are less obvious—but perhaps no less hazardous—when applied to close friends and family members.

Funny things happen when you are dealing with someone you know well; you don't examine them quite as closely, you very rarely look twice and, even if you do, you tend not to refine your judgements. You just assume that, "Mom is Mom, and will always be Mom." The trouble is that you may be wrong; Mom may not be who you think she is. You might be seeing one piece of her, and assuming that piece is indicative of the rest (as Kimberly did with her grandfather—he was too old to run, so therefore he couldn't play cards). Or you might be picturing her as she once was, rather than as she is now (as Andrew's mother did). Or you might just be wrong (as Sandy was about her sister-in-law). It's easy to do, difficult to undo, and crucial to avoid.

Discovering the true identity of the main characters in your life is a two-step process. First, you must determine who the specific members of the cast are: your mother, father-in-law, great aunt, spouse, child, etc. Then, you must look beneath your preconceived notions and uncover who they really are—not how you view them, but who they are in all their complexity and reality.

Completing *Awareness Exercise I* is a start toward helping you achieve this. If this, or any exercise, is not your style, skip it; if you don't have the time, just skim it for content and think about it when you are less harried.

Awareness Exercise I

1) Referring back to Page 32, the genogram of Gail Clark's family, develop a genogram of your own family. Use squares to indicate males, circles for females. Solid lines between figures mean marriage or parent-child ties; dotted lines indicate divorce. A diagonal line through a figure shows that individual has died. Place the name and age of each person inside the appropriate square or circle.

2) Using this *Awareness Exercise I* as a guide, make your own copy and place each living person in one of the four categories based on how often you have contact with them. Do you see or speak with them daily? weekly? monthly? less than once a month? If you are not sure, estimate more contact rather than less.

Awareness Exercise I: Family Contact

DAILY	WEEKLY	MONTHLY	LESS OFTEN

3) Those people whose names appear in the first three columns of your sheet can be considered the main characters in your Big Squeeze. Look at the names in these columns and ask yourself the following questions:

a) How many are there?
b) How does this make you feel?
c) Are there too many for you to handle?

4) In a 2-person group there is one relationship (one person to one person), in a 3-person group there are three relationships (each person has one relationship with each of the other two), in a 6-person group there are 15 relationships,

and in a 10-person group there are 45 relationships. Look at the names in your columns again and, once again, ask yourself the questions noted under Step 3.

* * * *

So now you know who your main characters are. And you have a fair idea of their relative potential for demand and/or support (roughly indicated by the amount of contact you have with them). You also may be getting your first inkling of why you have been feeling so overwhelmed.

You know their names, you know how often you see or talk to them, but do you know who they really are? *Awareness Exercise II* can help you begin to figure this out.

Awareness Exercise II

1) Take each of your main characters (those falling in the first three columns of your *Awareness Exercise I* sheet) and write a short description of them: strong points, weak points, physical strengths, physical weaknesses, likes, dislikes, past and present occupations, talents, hobbies, financial situation, potential demands, potential supports, etc.

2) Write the same description of the same people, but now, do it, first, from the point of view of their best friend, and then as they would describe themselves.

3) Compare the descriptions, and ask yourself the following questions:

> a) How different are each of the descriptions for each individual, and how do they differ?
> b) What does this tell you about your perceptions of your family? Are these perceptions realistic or affected by your own preconceived notions?
> c) What does this tell you about yourself and your family?
> d) How does all of this make you feel?

* * * *

Now you have a much more realistic picture of your cast: their names, how much time you spend with them, how important they are to you, your perception of who they are—and, most importantly, who they really are. Remember that each of these people is a potential source of support and/or demand. Remember that each can probably support you more, and demand less of you, than they are doing right now. And remember that these demands and supports will change over time.

Who are you, and where do you fit?

So that's who they are--but who are you? Where do you fit into the scheme? Where do you fit into your family system? You may see yourself as the director, responsible for managing and choreographing everyone else's moves. You may see yourself as the star, the center of your family system, affected by and affecting everything that goes on. Or you may see yourself as just another cast member, on equal footing with your siblings and parents. Perhaps you are now in the role of the director, but yearn for the day you might become a member of the cast.

Regardless of how you see yourself, true awareness starts with understanding who you are in your family—and why this is so. Once you begin to understand these things you will be better able to understand how these facts affect how you act—and how you feel about yourself and everyone else.

Are you the baby? Are you the eldest? Are you the one everyone turns to for support? Or are you the one everyone forgets about? Are you perceived by your family as competent or as bungling? The good guy or the bad guy? The cheap one of the spend-thrift? *Awareness Exercise III* may help you understand some of these complexities a little better.

Awareness Exercise III

1) Write a short description of yourself: strong points, weak points, physical strengths, physical weaknesses, likes, dislikes, past and present occupations, talents, hobbies, financial situation, potential demands, potential supports, etc.

2) Now write the same description but from the point of view—as appropriate—of your mother, your father, each of your siblings, your spouse, each of your children, any other family member you think would be useful.

3) Compare the descriptions and ask yourself the following questions:

a) How different are each of the descriptions of you? How do they differ?
b) Whose descriptions are the most positive? Whose are negative? Are you hardest on yourself, or are others?
c) What does this tell you about your family's perceptions of you? Are they realistic, or are they affected by their own preconceived notions?
d) What are the factors that might affect your family's notions? Birth order? Childhood behavior? Adult behavior?
e) What does this tell you about your family and their perception of your place within it?
f) What does this tell you about yourself, your perceptions of yourself, and your place within the family?
g) How does all of this make you feel?

* * * *

You may now be getting a more complete, more realistic picture of your family system. But this isn't all; there is more to your Big Squeeze than just your immediate family.

The Supporting Cast

Even in the long-ago days of the family farm, no family was an island unto itself, separate and self-sufficient. Even then, there were neighbors to help raise barns, peddlers hawking their wares, the church, the school, the feed store, the sheriff, the banker, and the local doctor. In contemporary modern society, life is much more complex, support and interaction circles much broader.

Your Big Squeeze can be altered, exacerbated, or eased by all the people, places, and things with which you have regular contact—and all the people, places and things with which your main characters have regular contact. Is it any wonder you are overwhelmed?

Awareness Exercise IV can help you become more alert to who and what else might be placing demands upon you, and who and what else might serve as a source of support.

Awareness Exercise IV

1) Make a list of up to 20 persons and institutions—excluding the family members listed in *Awareness Exercise I* —with whom you come in contact on a weekly basis. Include close friends, neighbors, co-workers, co-volunteers, community organizations, religious organizations, etc.

2) Make the same list—but only go to ten—for each of the family members in the first two columns of your *Awareness Exercise I* sheet (daily and weekly contact).

* * * *

When the results of this exercise are added to the results of *Awareness Exercise I* you will have a complete cast list; but knowing who all the players are is not enough. To fully understand what is going on you also need to be aware of the underlying themes and issues that motivate your—and their—behavior.

The Complicating Emotional Issues

In addition to its practical problems and concerns, the Big Squeeze also involves a wide array of emotional issues. The aging of a parent opens a Pandora's box of fears and concerns —fears and concerns you are probably spending a lot of time and energy avoiding. Loss. Death. Their aging. Your aging. Repaying the parental debt. Sending messages to your children. Needing to be needed. Failure. Child-parent role reversal.

These things are frightening, nebulous, and difficult to face. But if you don't face them, if you pretend that they aren't there, they will come back to haunt you in any number of ways. You may pull away when you really want to be close. You may be controlling and full of angry oversolicitiousness, when all you really want is to be a good child. You may constantly find fault. You may play Pollyanna. You may deny. You may rebel. You may become overinvolved.

If you treat your mother like your child, she may become so angry that your relationship is destroyed. If you refuse to talk with your father about his impending death—under the mistaken belief that if you don't talk about it, then it won't happen—you will never find out who he really wanted to get his favorite fishing pole, and you may never get to say goodbye. If you attempt to right previous wrongs by trying to make your mother's final months the best of your relationship, you are setting yourself up to fail.

Where there is no acknowledgement there can be no growth. You will be stuck. You will stagnate—or worse, you will be ineffective. But if you acknowledge these issues, and face them directly, you have a chance to deal with them and control how they affect your behavior; if you ignore and deny them, they control you.

Loss and death

How often have you heard praise for the woman who goes right back to work after her mother's death, or heard whispers of derision in reference to the man who just can't seem to bounce back after the loss of his brother? American society plays down the importance of grieving and puts many obstacles in the way of necessary mourning behavior; if this is the case after a death, what does that tell you about the cultural norms for behavior *before* someone has died?

* * * *

Marge Gleason was explaining to her friend Nan how upset she was with her father's worsening arthritis and growing hostility. She was agitated and weepy as she described how he had yelled at her for trying to help him open a jar.

"Calm down," Nan tried to console her. "You're making this into too big a deal—and making yourself crazy to boot. Relax. He's just getting a little difficult in his old age. What can you do? Everyone ages—be glad he's still alive."

"I suppose you're right," Marge said, staring out the window. "But somehow it doesn't make me feel any better."

* * * *

Marge didn't feel better because Nan's advice was wrong; it *is* a big deal. It's a big deal because a parent's decline is indicative of so much more: loss, death, fear of his death, fear of the unknown, fear of your death.

You know it's the beginning of the end: he's losing his health, his memory, his gusto, perhaps his independence; you are losing the strong man who has always been there for you, and the generation that stood between you and old age—between you and death. Or you may be mourning the loss of your last chance at having the mother you always wanted, or grieving because now you know for sure you will never get the love and acceptance you always craved from your father but never received. And your parents are most likely feeling similar—if not greater—sorrow, regret, and devastation.

You are all grieving for current and future losses; but no one—including you—really allows you to mourn. So the emotions become jumbled and convoluted, and may make you act in ways that you don't understand.

In theory, Elisabeth Kubler-Ross' five stages of anticipatory grief are widely accepted:[6]

1) denial and shock;
2) anger and irritability;
3) bargaining;
4) depression and beginning acceptance;
5) true acceptance.

Her theories are so accepted that others have built upon her work and hypothesized anticipatory grief stages for different situations. For example, when death is probable but not certain:

1) shock;
2) anger;
3) grief and anticipatory grief;
4) bargaining;
5) a period of uncertainty;
6) a favorable outcome leading to renewal and rebuilding—or
7) an unfavorable outcome leading to the Kubler-Ross stages above.

And when the loss doesn't necessarily lead to death:

1) recognition of the painful reality of the impending loss;
2) denial;
3) replacement of reality with a more tolerable situation;
4) yielding to some aspect of the loss;
5) intermittent denial;
6) resolution of conflicts;
7) reorientation and reconstitution of a new reality.

6. Kubler-Ross, Elizabeth. *On Death and Dying.* New York: McMillan, 1970.

Unfortunately, these stages are much more readily accepted in theory than they are in fact; those experiencing an impending loss are often discouraged from discussing or expressing their feelings. But the truth is, despite the messages you are getting from others, you are most likely going through some kind of the anticipatory grieving. Determining where you are in the process can help you understand your motivations and behaviors—and help you deal more effectively with the stresses of your life.

Are you buying plane tickets to visit your mother in Florida next winter when the doctor told you she probably won't live until fall? Denial. Are you picking fights with your father, because you think that if you are angry it won't hurt so much when he dies? Replacement. Are you at your mother-in-law's every day because you figure if you take really good care of her, then she won't die? Bargaining. Are you yelling at your husband for not mowing the lawn, when you could care less about the height of the grass? Anger and irritability. Think about it.

Repaying the parental debt

Some people think they owe their parents a tremendous amount; others think they owe less. Most likely, because you are reading this book, you fall into the former category. But it is important for you to realize that everyone owes their parents far more than can ever be repaid—for everyone owes their parents their life. Therefore, it is impossible to fully repay the parental debt; in trying, you only set yourself up to fail.

Whether you are attempting to repair a bad relationship, or striving to achieve the parental approval you never received, or responding to life-long love and nurturing, the *repaying* behavior is remarkably similar for all: a magnification of the importance of the final stage of your parent's life.

A magnification that often manifests itself in taking too much control, over-involvement, and burn out.

* * * *

> "I'm going to make Mom's last months the best ever!" cries the daughter who moved across the continent to get away from the mother she never really liked.
>
> "If I take really good care of Dad now, maybe he'll finally see that I'm not as dumb as he always thought," says the son whose father refused to send him to college because his grades weren't as good as his older brother's.
>
> "Mom was always there for me and I'm going to be there for her—for every last minute of her life."

* * * *

These three adult children may think they have the best of intentions, but the truth is they are all wrong. To the daughter who moved away: if you haven't been able to make it good before this, you can't make it good now. To the ill-treated son: you can't right all of life's wrongs in a short and finite period of time. To the appreciative child: if it has always been good, there are better ways to show your gratitude than taking control and overextending yourself.

So, if this type of repaying behavior won't fulfill your desired end, what will it get you? Burn out: you will get worn down, exhausted, and discover that there just isn't enough of you to go around. The result: you will be able to actually give less.

This is not to say that you shouldn't try to make your parent's final days as comfortable and pleasant as possible; just make sure that you pace yourself. Try to understand why it is important for you to do this; separate your underlying wishes from your behavior. Set reasonable expectations and appropriate limits to conserve your energy. You and your energy are finite.

Awareness Exercise V

1) Ask yourself the following questions:

   a) If you knew your parent was going to die next month, what would you do differently?
   b) If you knew your parent was going to live for another ten years, what would you do differently?
   c) If you knew your parent was going to outlive your spouse, what would you do differently?

2) Review your answers to the above questions and ask yourself:

   a) What facts can you be sure of?
   b) Do the answers change how you think you should live?
   c) Should you be prioritizing your time differently?
   d) Is there a balance that could be found?

* * * *

Role reversal: myth or reality?

Many people mistakenly view the declines and losses of aging as a regression to infancy. They assume their parents' increased difficulties eating, walking, and going to the bathroom are an indication that the roles have become reversed: child is now parent, parent is now child.

But the elderly are *not* children; they are adults. Adults who are used to taking care of themselves. Adults with a lifetime of accumulated wisdom. Adults with pride and dignity. Adults who will resent and fight you every inch of the way if you try to deprive them of their independence and self-esteem.

When you wiped cereal from little Johnny's mouth, he was oblivious to your caretaking activities and was only concerned with the way your necklace sparkled in the sun. But when you wipe cereal from your mother-in-law's mouth, she is aware; it is the stroke that keeps her from feeding herself. Her mind may be as acute and active as it ever was, and she has a long history of taking care of herself. Put yourself in her place, how would you want your children to treat you?

Your parent is not your child. Aging may have a few outward manifestations similar to childhood, but the inner experience is completely different. Your father may need some help in the kitchen, or may need you to drive him to the doctor, but that doesn't make him a child. If your wife broke her leg skiing and needed you to drive her to work, would you consider her child? If your sister's surgery kept her in bed and you brought her family dinner for a week, would you consider her a child? Well, your father is no more a child than your wife or your sister.

One of the most unfair and unnecessary losses of aging in America is loss of self-esteem. Retirement, self-sufficient children, decreased financial resources, physical infirmities that cut down on hobbies and social activities, and a society that idolizes youth all work together to deprive the elderly of a sense of status and self-importance. When you treat your mother as if she were a child, you exacerbate an already unjust situation—and may actually facilitate her decline.

And so, since *your parents are not your children,* shouldn't they be allowed to retain the power to take care of themselves and make their own decisions to the greatest extent possible, for as long as possible? Shouldn't they be allowed to keep what is still theirs, when they have already lost so much? You may find that the less power you usurp, the happier they will be, the better your relationship will be, and—as an extra bonus—the less stressed you will feel.

Sending messages to your children

How often have you heard your father's words come from your mouth when you discipline your son? How often have you listened to your husband speaking to your daughter and heard his mother's voice? It is a well-established fact that, in most cases, children parent the way they were parented. What is seen and heard, what is observed in a parent's behavior, is a powerful model for values and behaviors in later life.

Keep asking yourself if you are treating your mother the way you wish your children to treat you when you are your mother's age. Every time the answer is *no*, loop back to this step and ask yourself why you are doing it.

Needing to be needed

It has been estimated that the average American woman will spend at least 17 years taking care of her children, and at least 18 years taking care of elderly parents. Although male/female role distinctions are becoming less clear-cut, it is still a fact that the majority of nurturing in the United States is done by women. Some women do it out of habit, some out of obligation, and some out of desire. It is important to understand the reasons behind this nurturing behavior. Do we take care of our mothers because we want to, because we have to, or because we need to?

For those who have grown to define themselves as nurturers, this can be a difficult issue. The woman whose children are growing up—leaving or soon to leave the nest—may turn to an aging father as a replacement. She may delude herself as to the extent of her father's need, take control of his life, and drive him crazy with her constant interference. She may exhaust herself, and alienate him, for no reason.

What about you? Are you nurturing because you need to be a caretaker, or are you nurturing because they need to be cared for?

It's okay to nurture; it's wonderful to give of yourself to care for another human being—and nurturing need not only be doing *for,* nurturing can also be doing *with.* So go ahead and nurture—just make sure that you are doing it for the right reasons. And make sure you are doing it for, or with, someone who needs it.

Fear of failure

One of the overriding worries of those who care for aging parents is the fear that they will fail—fail the parent, and fail themselves. One of the best indicators of whether you will perceive yourself as a success or as a failure, is how you define these words.

Do you define success in terms of your parent's happiness? I can make Dad love the Senior Center. Or in terms of your parent's acquiescence? It's up to me to get Mom to take her medicine. Or in terms of your parent's health and recovery? It's my job to help Jeff's father regain the use of his leg—and I will—I will walk with him everyday. Or, perhaps the worst case, do you define success as victory over death? My love and attention will keep Mom alive.

You can't make Dad love the Senior Center. You can't make Mom take her medicine. You can't make Jeff's father walk again. And you can't keep death away forever. Your success or failure as a human being—or as a son or daughter—can't depend upon winning a game you are destined to lose. Aging and death are absolutes—and they will always win in the end.

STEP 2
Expectations

Where It Ends Up

The two telephone conversations that follow were going on simultaneously in Sharon, Massachusetts one fall afternoon.

* * * *

> "I just don't know what to do," Sherry Gilbert told her friend Michelle. "Ever since Dad died, Mom's been having Friday-night dinner with us. At first I didn't mind—I could tell it helped her to be around the kids—but now I'd really like to have my Friday nights back. I know I'm being selfish, but we used to have such nice, quiet evenings, just Alex and me and the kids .... But Mom expects to come, and looks forward to it all week. It would kill her if I ever suggested she skip it."
>
> "I just don't know what to do," Edie Bander said to her friend Shirley. "Sherry has been so wonderful since Harold died; she and the kids have really been a great source of comfort to me. But now I'm ready to be on my own. Lois wants me to join their dinner-bridge night, but it's on Friday and I know that Sherry expects me for dinner every Friday night. It means so much to her, and I know if I stopped coming she would think it was because of the children's bickering."

* * * *

Expectations and pretense

Who expects—and really wants—what from whom? And how accurate are these expectations? Sherry doesn't want her mother to come for dinner every Friday night, but Edie thinks her daughter expects it. Edie doesn't want to be invited to dinner every week, but Sherry thinks she expects it. Both women think they know what the other wants and expects, but they are both wrong. And because neither wants to hurt the other's feelings, they will go on having Friday night dinner together—and sometimes having to pretend to enjoy it—when they would each rather be doing something else.

* * * *

Rachel Grant finally got up the courage to make an appointment with her high school guidance counselor. The tearful girl confessed that she was unable to understand her chemistry class and was failing; she was receiving a "C" on her report card next week. Rachel knew that her father would be enraged; he expected her to get all "A's"—especially in chemistry—and to go to medical school to be a doctor just like him.

The guidance counselor set up tutoring sessions for Rachel and called her parents. Al Grant was amazed; he was sure that he had no expectation that Rachel get all "A's"—or go to medical school. He had just recently told her not to study so hard, and to spend more time enjoying her artistic talents.

But now that it was mentioned, Al wondered what unconscious messages he might be sending to Rachel, and what he really did expect of her.

* * * *

How does it get so convoluted? How is it that people who love each other, and talk often to each other, can develop such erroneous ideas about what each expects?

Your expectations color your actions and the messages these actions send to others, both indirectly and directly, Similarly, others' behavior may be reflective of the messages they receive from you. Therefore, your inappropriate expectations may not only affect *your* behavior, but can boomerang mistaken messages back at you through others' erroneous expectations for you—expectations they picked up from your own erroneous expectations for yourself. And this works both ways.

For example, if you expect yourself to visit your mother every day, your sister will expect you to also—and probably won't go herself. If your father expects you to pay for his full-time aide, you will probably expect yourself to do it also —even though you know the money is coming from your children's college fund. If your daughter expects you to be a Girl Scout leader because that's what you promised before you went back to work and your mother got sick, you will probably arrange to leave work early on Girl Scout days, ask your mother to spend Tuesday afternoons at the Senior Center instead of with you, and—perhaps—burn yourself out.

Expectations are powerful motivators, and their power is enhanced by their interactive effects—a power that can cause devastating consequences if the underlying expectations are not understood and addressed.

When expectations match—and when they don't

It is unfortunately a rare case where everyone's expectations match, or where everyone's abilities equal those expectations. If what they expect meshes with what you want and are able to give—great. But what happens when there is no match between your wants and expectations and theirs? And what happens when there isn't even a match between your own?

What happens when what they expect matches what you wish you could give, but not with what you are able to give? What happens when your mother expects you to remain in a marriage that you wish you could live with, but can't? You feel guilty and she feels disappointed.

What happens when what they expect doesn't match what you want to give? What happens when your father expects you to visit him weekly, but you don't want to because of the way he ignored you when you were a child? You feel angry and resentful, and so does he (perhaps with a little hurt underneath).

And what happens when your own expectations don't match what you can give? What happens when your desire to help your mother through her grief over the loss of your father is impossible because you are in such a depressed state of mourning yourself? You feel guilty and miserable, and she feels just as bad.

Or how about the situation where your own expectations are mutually exclusive? What happens when your expectation to be a good wife—to put your spouse and your children first—comes into conflict with your expectation to be a good daughter or son—to sacrifice time with your husband and kids to support your parents? What happens when, by definition, being the best at one means being at least a partial failure at the other? You feel guilty and miserable, your self-esteem plummets, and you perceive that you are letting everyone down—including yourself.

This need not be the case. For if you understand where the expectations come from, and how they differ from wishes and hopes, you will be able to avoid some of these emotional pitfalls.

The difference between wishes, hopes, and expectations

Wishes and hopes are often very different from expectations, and if you understand and acknowledge this you will be well on your way toward your goal of balance, because you cannot let your actions be based on wishes and hopes that will most likely never come true. Your father will never be Robert Young—no matter how much you wish it. Your mother will never be carefree if she has been a worrier all her life.

What you wish and hope is often not what you really expect to occur. You *wish* your mother didn't have cancer. You *hope* the doctors are wrong—or that they discover a miracle cure. But you really—deep down in your heart of hearts—*expect* she will only live until spring.

If your behavior is based on your wishes and hopes—if you pretend that what you wish and hope is really what you expect—you will take the wrong actions. You will not discuss important matters with your mother. You will not prepare your father for her death. You will not prepare yourself for your impending loss.

Sometimes it is hard to let go of the world as you have idealized it—as you wish it were. The images you wish for your parents, or your children, or for yourself are hard to release. Sometimes these images are based on false premises or are modeled on fictional movie or TV characters. Sometimes they are completely unreal, and sometimes they are close enough to reality to be easily confused with expectations. But until you can clearly see the differences between your wishes and your expectations you will have difficulty achieving the balance you need.

Who expects what, from whom, and why

You may not be able to control all the expectations that surround you—including your own—but if you can discover what some of them are, where they come from, and how they interrelate, you will be better able to act clearly and rationally. For the more you know, the better you will be at understanding what motivates everyone's behavior. This increased understanding and sensitivity will enable you to act in ways that more accurately reflect your true feelings, thereby enhancing your ability to make decisions and initiate change while decreasing the chances that others will incorrectly read your messages.

What do you expect from yourself, and why? Are these realistic and valid expectations given the situation today? What do your parents expect from you? Are their expectations reasonable? And what about everyone else's? Are their expectations what they really expect, or what you have lead them to believe they can expect from you? Where do all these expectations come from—and which ones are real?

Where It Came From

Some expectations are good: you expect yourself to be an honest and reliable worker. Some expectations are bad: you expect your son to become a concert pianist because that is what you always wanted to be. Some expectations were good at one time, but aren't appropriate any longer: always being there for your mother was fine when she only called on you three times a year, now that she calls three times a day your expectations and definitions of *dutiful daughter* have to change. Where do these expectations come from, and why are they so powerful?

Expectations come from a variety of sources, some are messages you received as a child growing up in a particular society, some are things that were expected of you as a member of your unique family, and some are individual ideals you have developed for yourself. It is impossible to understand what motivates your—and everyone else's—behavior without looking at the derivation of the expectations that underlie that behavior.

The mythical American family

Contemporary American society is full of messages about how you should be. You shouldn't have dandruff. You should drive a shiny new car. You shouldn't let your kitchen floor get dirty. You should have obedient children, a happy spouse, and spry parents who play tennis daily, visit the Orient, and babysit at a moment's notice.

But the truth is, it just ain't so. There is real life, and there are the *shoulds* the media perpetuate every day. It is virtually impossible for an active member of American society to avoid the media; and the messages heard since childhood form a layer of attitudes, feelings, and beliefs. These beliefs may be buried under tiers of skepticism, cynicism, or intellectual denial, but they are still there. And they color your expectations about who you, and the people around you, should be.

* * * *

They are all gathered in front of a tall, glittering Christmas tree: a joyful mid-life couple surrounded by radiant brothers and sisters and children and nieces and nephews; a youthful set of grandparents stand proudly off to the side. The husband and wife smile deep into each others' eyes; the woman rises and places a box overflowing with long-stemmed roses in her mother's arms. Her siblings join her; all gaze at the older woman (although she looks barely 50) with love and reverence. "When it comes from the heart, say it with flowers," intones the voice-over.

* * * *

Claire and Cliff Huxtable are throwing a surprise anniversary party for Cliff's parents. His parents enter, spry and silly, masks on their faces, teasing their son and daughter-in-law. Claire's parents, two of Claire and Cliff's children and one of their grandchildren are all at the party. Four generations share, hug, kiss, laugh, and put on a musical play together.

* * * *

There are no tensions. No one is really old. No one is sick. The family is alive and well on national TV.

And if it's not Madison Avenue or Bill Cosby's perfect family, perhaps it's the archetypal superwoman on "Who's the Boss," or the way complex intergenerational problems get tied up into a tidy solution in less than 30 minutes on "Charles in Charge."

Is it any surprise that you hold unrealistic expectations for your parents, your children, and yourself when these are the messages you have heard every day of your life? Is it any surprise that, in the back of your mind, you think you should be smiling like Donna Reed, while handing lunch boxes to hubby and clean-faced children as they leave in the morning?

Or do you periodically experience pangs of guilt because you aren't home baking cookies the way June Cleaver always did? Or do you feel bad because you aren't a hot-shot lawyer like Claire Huxtable? Or because your toilet bowl doesn't sparkle? Or because your arthritic father bears no resemblance to Bill Cosby's healthy and active one? Or because your problems don't get neatly solved in 30-minute segments?

Perhaps your expectations are based on Hollywood rather than reality.

The norm of politeness

Your mother is dying. Your bad knee feels like it's on fire. And the guidance counselor at the high school just called to discuss your son's excessive absences—absences you weren't even aware of. You walk into your office and one of your co-workers asks how you are. You smile, tears pricking at the back of your eyes, and say you are fine. You expect yourself to keep your personal life separate from your work life. You expect yourself to protect others from unpleasantness. You want to avoid the pain of disclosure. Perhaps, you think, if you ignore it, it will go away and it won't hurt so much.

These expectations and defenses may be appropriate and helpful in some situations, particularly situations where the problems are minor or out of your control. But if you deny or try to avoid a problem that demands action, you aren't protecting anyone—least of all yourself. Your expectation of what is appropriate and polite behavior may be exacerbating your problems and prolonging your agony.

The idealized self

Often, adult children set expectations for themselves that are based on how they were parented: what they want to *pay back*; what they feel they must or should do; or what they need to prove to themselves or their parents. These expectations usually have nothing to do with what the parent really wants or needs—or what the adult child is capable of giving.

* * * *

Sally Amann shifted in the hard chair that was pushed up against the side of her father's bed. She touched the papery skin of the elderly man's hand, but there was no response. She knew there wouldn't be; her father hadn't responded to anything in the outside world for at least three months. The doctors said he probably never would. But Sally came every day and sat by the bedside—just in case.

To do so she had to give up her evening hours with the family—she left Paul to scrounge dinner for himself and the kids from the freezer or the local pizza parlour, and she was exhausting herself in the bargain. She knew her father would never want her to neglect her family or jeopardize her health, but Sally couldn't help it. Her father had always been there for her, and she would be there for him.

* * * *

Edward Zych stared around the stark and sterile room his mother shared with three other elderly women. The whole thing disgusted and upset him, all four of them revolted him: the woman near the window in a coma, whose position had never varied in the year he had been coming here; the overly-friendly one, who always told him how handsome he was; the one surrounded by so many family pictures the nurses could never get close to her bed; and his mother, angry and bitter, her left side paralyzed by a stroke. He glared at his mother; she glared back and said nothing.

They often said nothing during his bi-weekly visits. He knew his mother didn't care if he came—she probably would prefer if he didn't—but he was determined to prove himself better than the mother who had neglected him for her adored second husband. He was better than she. He would show her.

* * * *

It is crucial to be clear about the motivations that underlie your behavior, for only when you see these expectations and motivations for what they are, can you be rational about the best course of action.

Expected family roles

The way things were in the past has a strong effect on how people expect things to be in the present—even if those patterns and roles don't make sense anymore. The role that you had as a child—the nurturer, the *doer*, Dad's favorite—is often the role expected of you as an adult. This may hold true even if the circumstances, or your personality, don't fit that role anymore—perhaps they never did.

In almost all families there is a single child who takes on the role of the *responsible one:* the one who assumes primary responsibility for the parent needing care. The reason an individual is chosen often reflects their childhood role, their sex (female), their geographical proximity to the parent, or their expectations for themselves based on these things. When these expectations are in line with reality, the situation is positive—where the expectations and reality are misaligned, anger, resentment, and burnout can ensue.

* * * *

Carla Tomasello was beside herself. The eldest daughter in a family of six—three brothers, herself, and a sister who refused to have anything to do with her parents—Carla's brothers had *sent* their mother out to live with her after the older woman's heart attack. It didn't matter that Carla had a husband and three children. It didn't matter that their house was too small. It didn't matter that her brother Dom had no children and two guest rooms. Carla was the daughter and everyone knew daughters were expected to care for their mothers. The whole family agreed—except Carla's husband Vince.

After two months of caring for her mother, fighting with Vince, and screaming at the kids, Carla was beginning to think her husband might be right; but every time these thoughts crossed her mind she pushed them away. She couldn't exactly tell her brothers to "take Mom back." No, she knew her place in the family. This was the way it was supposed to be.

* * * *

Carla is a victim of her own and her brothers' expectations —all based on her birth order, her role in the family, *and* her sex. There is no denying that woman are the primary nurturers in contemporary American society; there is also no denying that this fact has much more to do with expectations than it has to do with ability.

When it comes to caring for elderly parents, women shoulder an overwhelming percentage of the responsibility (over three-quarters of primary care-givers to the elderly are women), and it is almost always a woman who becomes the *responsible one.* Often this is because women have learned to expect it of themselves, or because their male relatives expect it of them. Where it is appropriate, desired, and possible, it is good. When this is not the case, the caretaking role is, by definition, coerced, and this cannot be good.

Nurturing is not the exclusive domain of women, nor is caring for a parent a job done best by one person. But these are both things that can happen when the underlying expectations are not explored, not understood, and not changed when they are inappropriate.

What Can You Do?

So, what can you do? You can recognize what the expectations are, and where they come from. You can acknowledge their existence. You can choose not to buy into erroneous ones. You can decide on a reasonable set of expectations for yourself.

Unfortunately, your ability to directly impact others' expectations is probably quite limited, but recognition and acknowledgement of both their, and your own expectations, can have strong positive effects. For even if you can't meet them, being aware is a start toward more honest communication and, hopefully, increased mutual understanding.

It isn't easy to keep yourself from buying into other's incorrect, ineffective, or manipulative expectations of you—or of your own misguided expectations for yourself. In order to choose what to expect of yourself, and to confront the difference between what you expect and what others expect of you, you have to deal with the underlying expectations—they often come in layers—that your family will be angry with you if you don't meet their view of who you should be and how you should act.

And this may be a source of concern for you: for if you don't do what they want, might not you lose their love and approval? Is this worth the risk? Maybe you can answer this question by asking another: what is the risk on the other side? The alternate risk is that you lose something of yourself. Is this worth it? Maybe you can answer this question by looping back to step 1, Awareness.

Recognizing overt and covert expectations

In every interaction between people there are two sets of messages: the overt and the covert. In this case, the overt messages are the expectations that are directly communicated, and the covert messages are the expectations that are hidden—sometimes deeply and sometimes very close to the surface—underneath the actions or the spoken words.

Sometimes the two messages are the same. For example, when you tell your daughter that if she doesn't get dressed in five minutes she will miss the bus, your message on both levels in the same: "I expect you to get dressed, and I expect you to catch the bus."

Sometimes, the two messages are quite different. For example, when your husband asks you to cancel your tutoring session to take his mother to the doctor because he has a meeting, his overt message might be, "I expect you to help me because we are a family," but covertly he might be saying, "I expect you to help me because my work is more important than yours," or "Because you are a woman, I expect you to do the caretaking." Your response to his request may have more to do with his covert expectations than with the words he is saying, and the result may be misunderstanding and disagreement, with resentment and anger on both sides. For even if neither party is consciously aware of the underlying expectations, these expectations have a way of coming through—and of confusing the meaning of the resulting behavior and increasing everyone's level of stress.

Therefore, there should be three goals:

1) Make your covert and overt messages as similar as possible;
2) Where this is impossible, be as honest about them as you can;
3) Identify the covert expectations underlying the messages of others, so that your behavior is as straight forward as possible.

* * * *

When Adam Belmonte reached his office he called to check-in with his mother—as he did every morning. "I'm a little weak," the older woman told her son. When Adam suggested that he hire someone to come in for a few hours to help around the house, his mother replied in a soft voice, "Oh no, I'm fine. Just fine. I don't need a stranger around the house."

* * * *

Zelda Yager put everything on hold and spent the morning running errands for her father. She went food shopping, picked up his medications at the pharmacy, met with the director of the congregate meal site about the problem he had had during lunch the previous week, and picked up the forms he needed from the housing office. She had to wait at every stop, and it was past noon by the time she reached her father's apartment. He was profuse with his thanks as she straightened up the living room, made his bed, and put away the groceries. But she was way behind on her own chores and errands.

"Busy, busy, busy," her father said wistfully as she headed out the door. "It's nice that your life is so full. If only you had a few moments so we could have a nice little talk."

* * * *

Bonnie Cohen wanted to spend Hanukkah with her sister's family; her husband Mike wanted to go skiing. Bonnie told her husband that she would take the children to her sister's, he could invite some friends up to Vermont and ski. That way everyone would be happy. Mike was skeptical. "No, no, I won't be angry," Bonnie assured him. "I didn't get to see my family over Thanksgiving because we were at your mother's, so I want to be with them now. But you don't need to. We're grown-ups: you do what you want, I'll do what I want." Mike went to Vermont; they bickered over the laundry, whether the kids needed to wear hats, and which movie to see for the entire month of January.

* * * *

Covert versus overt. In Adam's case, his mother's overt message was, "I'm fine. Perhaps a little tired, but I can manage." Her covert message was, "I expect you to help me and only you will do. If you aren't willing to help then I'll have to manage by myself—weak as I am." And most damaging, she was saying to him, "If you don't take care of me you aren't a good enough son."

In Zelda's case, her father's overt message was, "Thank you for all your help." His covert message was, "I expect you to spend more time with me. You aren't good enough."" And Bonnie was just kidding herself; clearly, her covert message was, "We visited *your* family over Thanksgiving, and I expect you to visit *mine* for Hanukkah."

Did Adam, Zelda, and Mike pick up the fact that there were covert messages and expectations being sent? You bet they did. Were their feelings hurt? Did they experience guilt? anger? confusion? You bet. Were the others aware of their underlying expectations and contradictory messages? It's difficult to be sure. But did the others feel hurt? guilty? a little angry? a little confused? You bet they did.

Making the covert messages clear is no guarantee that feelings won't be hurt—but at least the feelings will be dealt with as they happen rather than simmering under the surface.

It's complicated stuff. And it's complicating stuff. For hidden expectations—be they just or unjust, conscious or unconscious—have a way of displaying themselves, often as negative, covert messages; messages that the sender may be unaware of sending, but that the receiver is very aware of receiving. Therefore, if you are aware of your own expectations you will be better able to bring your covert and overt messages closer together. And, if you are aware of others' expectations, you will be better able to interpret their messages correctly and respond appropriately.

Again, this knowledge doesn't guarantee that everyone will be happy and that all will go smoothly. But the knowledge does increase your chances for mutual understanding and, hopefully, for better relationships: you will be more direct and you will have more compassion and understanding for the real feelings of others.

One of the ways to uncover some of your hidden expectations is to listen and look for the covert messages within your overt communications. *Expectation Exercise I* will help you achieve this by increasing your awareness of how your word choice, your inflection, your tone of voice, and your body language express feelings that might be far different from what you are saying.

This exercise needs to be repeated with a variety of people, and with the same people a number of times. The repetition will begin to give you clues as to how you express yourself covertly, and what the expectations underlying your covert communications might be.

Expectation Exercise I

1) Ask yourself the following simple set of questions the next few times you have a discussion with your parent, or your spouse, or your child:

a) What are you trying to say?
b) Do the words you are using say it the most directly? If not, why did you put it that way?
c) Are you using martyr language ("Oh, all right, I'll just have to do it myself.") or sighing a lot? If so, why?
d) Does your tone of voice match the sentiment you are trying to express? If not, why not?
e) Does your voice rise at the end of a statement, or stay level at the end of a question? If so, does this match what you are trying to say?
f) Is your voice smiling? frowning? whining? cajoling? angry? Is that what you feel?
g) Are you speaking in the same tone to your parents that you use for your children?
h) Are you clenching your teeth? making a fist? shaking your leg? drumming your fingers? If so, why might you be doing these things?

2) Now reflect on the answers above and ask yourself the following questions:

a) What do the answers tell you about what you are really feeling?
b) What do the answers tell you about the covert messages you might be sending?
c) Do these covert messages tell you anything about the underlying expectations you hold for yourself?
d) Are these expectations reasonable given the current situation?
e) Do these covert messages tell you anything about the underlying expectations you hold for the people with whom you are speaking?
f) Are these expectations reasonable given the current situation?
g) How might you begin to bring your covert and overt messages more in line with one another?

In the same way that *Expectation Exercise I* helped you determine where you might be sending mixed messages, and what your underlying expectations might be, *Expectation Exercise II* will help you determine the covert messages that may be underlying the expectations of others.

Expectation Exercise II

1) The next few times you have a discussion with your parent, or your spouse, or your child listen carefully to what they are saying and what they are implying, and watch their body language. Ask yourself the following questions:

a) What is she overtly trying to say?
b) Are the words she is using the words you would use to make her point? Why or why not?
c) Is she using martyr language or sighing a lot? If so, why?

d) Does her tone of voice match the sentiment you think she is trying to express? If not, why not?
e) Does her voice rise at the end of a statement, or stay level at the end of a question? If so, does this match what you think she is trying to say?
f) Is her voice smiling? frowning? whining? cajoling? angry? Is that what you think she is really feeling? If not, why not?
g) Is she clenching her teeth? making a fist? shaking her leg? drumming her fingers? If so, why might she be doing these things?

2) Now reflect on the answers above and ask yourself the following questions:

a) What do the answers tell you about what she is really feeling?
b) What do the answers tell you about the covert messages she is sending?
c) Do these covert messages tell you anything about the underlying expectations she holds for you?
d) Are these expectations reasonable given the current situation?
e) Do these covert messages tell you anything about the underlying expectations she holds for herself?
f) Are these expectations reasonable given the current situation?

Acknowledgement

Now that you are beginning to recognize some of the expectations underlying everyone's behavior, the next step is to acknowledge these expectations. It is not necessary that the expectations be rational, reasonable, or even have a possible solution; it is only necessary that they be granted existence. Acknowledging that an expectation exists—no matter how silly it is—goes a long way; sometimes it is even enough.

For example, perhaps *Expectation Exercise I* helped you recognize three of your own expectations:

1) You expect your mother to be a loving grandmother even though she has never been a loving person;
2) You expect yourself to be a loving mother and in your desire to prove this you are smothering your daughter's independence;
3) You expect yourself to be able to solve everyone's problems.

Acknowledge that these are your expectations, that they are real, and that they are based on valid feelings and desires.

There is nothing wrong with wishing that your mother were a loving grandmother, or wanting to be a loving parent yourself, or trying to make the troubles of those you love go away. These are valid, positive desires; they are an indication that you are a good, caring person. But, the question then arises, do valid desires make valid expectations? Again, there are important differences between desires, wishes, hopes, and expectations.

The process is similar for others, but in this case you need to acknowledge *their* expectations to *them.* Referring back to a previous example, if Adam Belmonte recognizes that his mother's expectation is that he be more available to her, he might say:

"Mom, I know you have been feeling lonely since Dad died, and that you would like me to spend more time with you—and I would like it, too. But we both know I can't. It's crummy. It stinks and I wish it weren't so--but it is. I love you, and I'll be with you as much as I can. But we both have to live with the fact that I need to work for a living."

They can now commiserate together; they have a common expectation that is not being met. Adam's mother will feel that her feelings are valid, and she might be less lonely knowing that she is understood; it is also possible that her martyr behavior may diminish. Adam may be surprised to find that he is not only enjoying her company more—he is also spending more time at her apartment.

It isn't always necessary to try to solve the problem that the expectation brings up; sometimes sympathy and acknowledgment of a difficult situation, or of discomfort, or of loneliness is enough. If your wife's father died you wouldn't try to *solve* her grief—you would acknowledge her loss, offer sympathy for her sadness, and do all you could to ease her pain. Often, the same is true of expectations.

Reasonable expectations

You have recognized and acknowledged the expectations, now you need to decide which expectations are reasonable, and which are not. Which expectations you can address, and which ones you cannot. And you need to start with your own. *Expectation Exercise III* is a first step.

Expectation Exercise III

1) Fill in the following statements as you would if you were speaking openly and frankly to a very close friend.

a) Whenever my mother __________, I ________.
b) Whenever I ___________, my mother _______.
c) Whenever my father ___________, I _________.
d) Whenever I __________, my father __________.
e) I wish ____________________________________.
f) It drives me crazy when ___________________.
g) I hate myself when _______________________.
h) Whenever my family gets together ___________.
i) I feel good about myself when ______________.

2) Review your answers and ask yourself the following questions:

a) What do your answers tell you about what you expect of yourself? Are these expectations reasonable?
b) What do your answers tell you about what you expect of your parents? Are these expectations reasonable?
c) Are there differences in the answers for the questions involving your father versus your mother? What does this tell you about your expectations for yourself in relation to either of them? What does it tell you about your relationship with either of them?
d) Are the feelings you state consistently positive? negative? neutral? What does your answer to this question represent to you?
e) Do you notice any patterns?
f) Overall, how reasonable are your expectations? How does the answer to this question make you feel?

It is the rare person whose life is a mirror of their expectations, whose ideal matches their real. But your goal is not to make your ideal, real; but rather to make your expectations reasonable in light of who you are, who they are, and the specific circumstances of your situation. You need to recognize the effects of your ideals and expectations on your behavior, keep the ones that work, integrate the ones that are possible, and let go of those that—for whatever reason—cannot be. You need to do this for the expectations that you hold for yourself, your parents, your spouse and your children; the primary goal is reasonable expectations for all.

Some of your expectations may have been possible and appropriate at a different time in your life, but are now unrealistic (exercising three times a week). Some of your expectations may have been fantasies right from the start (being independently wealthy and not having to work). And some of your expectations may be eminently reasonable and reachable (being a supportive daughter). Your job is to figure out which is which, and to develop a working compromise between your fantasy life and reality.

On the other side of this issue are the expectations others hold. Obviously, you have much less control over their expectations than you do over your own—and minimal ability to change them. But your knowledge and understanding of their expectations can change your reaction to them; and you may be surprised to find that this goes a long way. It will make you a better communicator, cut down on disagreements and misunderstandings, and increase your ability to deal appropriately with the situation.

As was true of your own expectations, others may also hold expectations that are unrealistic for the current situation, just plain fantasy, or that are eminently viable. You need to sort out which expectations fall into which categories, and respond to them as such.

And responding need not mean problem-solving. Responding may take the form of active listening, of offering sympathy, of expressing love and caring, or of honestly choosing not to respond.

If you recognize and acknowledge your expectations, you take some control of them. If you ignore or avoid them, they control you.

STEP 3
Needs

By definition, the Big Squeeze is about needs. It is about the neediness of the people in your life, and your ability—or inability—to meet their needs. It is about survival through effectively balancing everyone's needs—including your own.

But you can't begin to balance these needs until you recognize five things:

1) Which needs are real;
2) Which needs belong to whom;
3) Which needs you desire to meet;
4) Which needs you are able to meet;
5) Which needs might be met by others.

This chapter will focus on the first four issues, later chapters will deal with the fifth.

Needs, Desires, or Make Believe

Whose needs are these anyway?

Attributing your own feelings or attitudes to others (projection) is a very common human behavior. It is so common, in fact, that there is even a word—anthropomorphism—for attributing human abilities and feelings to animals.

Projection has a positive side; for example, if you see a homeless man huddled over a subway grate you can imagine how he must feel based on how you would feel in a similar situation; your understanding and compassion might motivate you to help him. But projection also has a negative side; for example, if you project your feelings or needs onto someone who does not share them.

* * * *

"Come on, Dad," Margaret Trubia said, holding her father's coat. "I only have half-an-hour before I need to pick up Jenny. So come on, you'll have a great time. Mr. Postell and Al Corsini will be there ..."

"I hate bowling," the elderly man grumbled as he put his arm in the sleeve.

"Now, now, Dad. What kind of talk is that?" Margaret patted his shoulder. "You can't stay in and read all the time, you know. It's not good for you. Not good for you at all."

"Maybe it's not good for *you*," he mumbled softly. "It's fine for *me*." But Margaret was already half way down the driveway and didn't hear him.

* * * *

"She needs to go away to college," Ed Debene told his wife Maria. "She has to."

"She doesn't want to," Maria replied.

"But she needs the experience—the worldliness. New people. New places. Excitement. All that stuff."

"She wants to stay here."

"She can't. Who wants to live at home and go to college? I would have hated living with my parents and seeing the same old places and faces at some local school."

"Ed, we live in one of the most exciting cities in the world. And she wants to go to Columbia—not East Oshkosh University!" Maria said.

Ed crossed his arms and glared at his wife. "She needs to go away to college."

Is it Margaret who needs to keep busy, or is it her father? Is it Ed who needs to go away to college, or is it his daughter? Sometimes it's hard not to project your needs onto others. Sometimes it's difficult to come to grips with the fact that the people you love—particularly those you take care of—often feel quite differently about things than you do. It isn't easy to recognize that they are unique, individual people, separate and distinct from you, or to acknowledge that their age and personality give them a different world view, or to realize that their needs and your needs might not be the same.

Need versus desire

Webster's defines *need* as a necessary duty: an obligation; and defines *desire* as the expression of a wish: a request. A need *must* be met, a desire *may* be met; this is a significant distinction. Unfortunately, it isn't always a clear distinction, as the line between need and desire is often blurred.

* * * *

"Mom, I need new skates or I'll never get the next skating badge."

"Honey, I need you to drive my mother to physical therapy on Tuesday—I'm completely jammed at work."

"Ron Sturgis' son takes him to church every Sunday. That's right—every Sunday."

"Sis, you're not working, can you run up to Dad's for me on Wednesday? I know it's my turn—and I know you covered for me last time—but I really need you to do this for me. Just one more time, please?"

* * * *

Does he *need* new skates? Does she *need* you to drive her mother? Does he *need* you at church every Sunday? Does she *need* you to go to your father's? Or are these just desires expressed as needs?

A need implies necessary acquiescence; a desire implies the possibility of refusal. Often you can choose to ignore or to meet the latter; you do not have the same latitude with the former. You know that. Your family knows that. Your boss knows that. Your friends know that. If you wanted something very badly, would you express it as a need or as a desire?

One of the ways to determine whether something is a need or a desire is to visualize the consequences of not meeting it. What would happen if you didn't buy him new skates? Didn't drive her mother? Didn't go to church with him on Sunday? Didn't visit your father? The answers to these questions will tell you a lot about whether something is really a necessity.

The problem of needs is often further complicated by the fact that what they may need or desire is not always in alignment with what you may need or desire. For example, your mother doesn't know how to fill out her Medicare forms and she needs you to do them for her. You aren't good at paperwork and you have a need to be competent in her eyes, or perhaps you hate paperwork and have a need to avoid it at all costs. So, where are you? You are sitting with a set of conflicting needs: yours versus hers. Perhaps what your mother really needs is to find someone else to fill out her forms—or maybe she needs to learn how to fill them out herself.

Sometimes the expression of needs as desires isn't purposeful. Sometimes a desire is unconsciously expressed as a need. Sometimes a desire is mistakenly perceived by the person to be a need. And sometimes, they really don't know which is which. If they can't tell the difference, it makes sense that it's a difficult task for you.

Surviving your Big Squeeze is dependent upon your ability to differentiate between real needs, perceived needs, and desires expressed as needs. Only then can you make a rational decision about *how* to meet the real needs and *whether* to meet the desires.

Of course, this differentiation is not easy. And it's made even more difficult by the fact that there are many reasons why you might hear a desire expressed as a need: he tells you this is what he needs; appearances indicate that this is what he needs; you think this is what he needs; or this is what you wish he needed.

So your ears and your eyes may be deceiving you. Or he may be deceiving you—consciously or unconsciously. Or you may be deceiving yourself—consciously or unconsciously. Understanding what you expect of yourself and knowing whether it is a need or a desire allows you to take appropriate action based on your own limits and feelings. You might want to loop back to steps 1 and 2 for help understanding these issues.

Needs Exercise I is another method that might help you figure out the scope and extent of everyone's real needs. Again, if this exercise is not your style, or if you feel it is too time-consuming, just skim it and go on.

Needs Exercise I

1) Refer back to your answers to *Awareness Exercises I and II* and put the name of every person who fell into the first three columns of *Awareness Exercise I* (your main characters) and those included on the first list of *Awareness Exercise II* (your supporting cast) on the top of a different sheet of paper. You now have a stack of paper with the names of all the important people and institutions who might be requesting something of you. Don't forget the household.

2) Based on your experiences over the past week, jot down:

a) The needs each of these people have expressed;
b) The needs you perceive;
c) The needs you have filled.

3) Review the lists and ask yourself the following questions:

a) Who or what brought this needs to your attention (yourself, the person in needs, someone or something else)?
b) Who perceived it as a need (you, the person, someone else)?
c) Why was it perceived as a need?
d) Is it a projection of someone else's need?
e) Is it a necessity or is it a request?

The answers to this exercise should begin to give you clues about the needs in your Big Squeeze that must be met (although not necessarily by you) and the issues for which there are options.

Volume

Their needs

The sheer volume of items you listed in the previous exercise probably caused you to question your ability—or anyone's ability—to meet the multiple demands in your life. This is a valid question. Most likely, it is an impossible feat; a feat that cannot be accomplished in the manner in which you have it currently structured—although it may be a feat that can be accomplished under a different set of assumptions. *Needs Exercise II* will help you start to assess the realistic possibility of meeting your current goals.

Needs Exercise II

1) Review your lists from *Needs Exercise I* and place all those pages that contain legitimate needs into one pile. For every person or institution that has a legitimate need, take a clean sheet of paper and, based on the chart below, make a new set of pages with the name of that person or institution on the top.

Needs Exercise II: Their Needs

NAME: ______________________

NEED	TIME/week	RANK	RESOURCES

2) Make a list of all the needs this person or institution has that you perceive, they perceive, or someone else perceives is partially or completely your responsibility to meet. Place these needs in the first column.

3) Estimate how much time it takes to meet each need in an average week (or across an average month and then divide by four) and record that figure in the second column.

4) Place a rank of 1 to 3 indicating the relative importance of that need (1 being the most important) in the last column.

5) Leave the last column, Resources, empty. You will complete that column as part of a later exercise.

Depending upon your specific situation, you may have three sheets or you may have twenty sheets. The next page shows an example of how your parent or in-law list might look.

NAME: Joe's Father's Needs

NEED	TIME/week	RANK	RESOURCES
Daily phone call	2 hours	1	
Lunch twice weekly	2 hours	2	
Sunday's family dinner	4 hours	1	
Making doctor's appts.	15 mins.	2	
Taking for haircut	15 mins.	3	
Weekly food shopping	1 hour	3	
Going to doctor	30 mins.	2	
Running errands	1 hour	3	
Taking to religious functions	1 hour	2	
Seeing movie together, etc.	3 hours	2	
Assisting w/financial affairs	1 hour	3	
Providing companionship		1	
Showing respect		1	
Showing love and approval		1	
Visiting with grandkids		1	

You will have a different set of lists than your friend Margie or the man down the street, and a different set of needs will be recorded on each sheet. But the chances are, each of you will have itemized more needs than you can possibly meet. And these aren't all the needs in your Big Squeeze. What about your own needs?

Are you always last?

You have just completed a series of needs lists, one each for all the important players in your life (your parents, in-laws, spouse, children, job, friends, household, etc.). Looking at these lists you probably feel overwhelmed—by a responsibility that is real: a responsibility to help and support those you care about.

But the question arises: how can you be there for them, if you aren't there for yourself? If you aren't meeting your own basic needs, it will be very difficult for you to meet theirs. This is not to say that you don't have a responsibility to them—you do, but for your sake, and theirs, you have a responsibility to yourself also.

* * * *

Iris Dobie was one of those people that everyone called in an emergency. And whenever she was called, she responded gladly with whatever was needed. It didn't matter if it was her sister, a neighbor she barely knew, or her daughter's Sunday school teacher. She was chair of the middle school's Spring Festival, active in her local League of Women Voters, and invaluable to the United Way's fund-raising campaigns. She was also mother to three children, wife to a busy executive, and daughter to a 75-year-old father who was growing more frail by the day.

Iris didn't have time to exercise or to see the doctor about the pains she was having. "Gas, or perhaps ulcers," she thought as she chewed antacids by the handful—even though they didn't help all that much.

When her father fell and Iris took him to the hospital, it was Iris they admitted, rather than her father. She collapsed in the waiting room, and they had to rush her into by-pass surgery to save her life. She was laid up for a month and was unable to settle her father into a nursing home, had to miss her daughter's dance recital, and the family was forced to cancel its summer vacation.

* * * *

Iris may be an extreme example, but she is also a valid example of what can happen if you make the mistake of forgetting about your own needs—or of placing your needs far behind those of others. But you don't need to be risking your health to say *no* and slow down—perhaps you're simply feeling the stress of an overloaded, unbalanced life.

You may not experience a heart attack, but all kinds of mental and physical illnesses are related to stress—from the common cold to hypertension to depression and chronic fatigue. This *back seat* attitude—combining the multiple stresses of meeting everyone else's needs with a lack of concern for your own—can, at a minimum, reduce your effectiveness or, at a maximum, incapacitate you.

Needs Exercise III is designed to help you determine if you are relegating your needs to the back of the bus. In the first part of this exercise you are asked to develop a needs list of your own. When you have completed your list, you will be able to sit in the middle of the floor and place all the lists in a semi-circle in front of you. You literally will be surrounded by the universe of needs squeezing you. The impact of this visual squeeze is extremely powerful and also can be extremely enlightening.

The second part of the exercise focuses on the way you view, value, and meet your own needs in comparison with how you view, value, and meet other people's needs.

Needs Exercise III

The directions for the first part of this exercise are similar to the directions for *Needs Exercise II*.

1) Using the chart below as a guide, list your own needs in the first column. The list on the next page contains general categories that might help you develop your list. Don't dismiss a category without fully exploring whether it does indeed apply to you (i.e. just because you don't enjoy jogging or aerobics doesn't mean that allocating time to exercise isn't a need). What else do you need that is not included on this list?

Needs Exercise III: Your Needs

NEED	TIME	SOURCE	RANK	RESOURCE

Categories of Potential Self-Needs

PRACTICAL	EMOTIONAL
Exercise	Time alone
Grooming	Privacy
Sleep	Attention
General health needs	Receiving love
Interests/Hobbies	Receiving acceptance
Companionship	Self-acceptance
Entertainment	Autonomy
Making a living	Intimacy
Housework	Financial success
Financial chores	
Childcare	
Home repairs	

2) Estimate how much time meeting each need takes in an average week (or across an average month and then divide by four) and record that figure in the second column.

3) Place a rank from 1 to 3 indicating the relative importance (1 being most important) of that need in the last column.

4) You will notice that there is one additional column that was not on your previous lists: Source. Place the names of the people (yourself, boss, spouse, friend, etc.) who might be able to fill this need for you in the third column. There can be more than one source for a single need.

5) As in *Needs Exercise II,* leave the resource column empty. You will fill this in during a later exercise.

6) After you have completed your list, review it and answer the following questions:

a) Who is the most common source listed for meeting your needs? Who is the source most often successful in meeting your needs? Who is the source least often successful in meeting your needs? What does this tell you about yourself?

b) How many of your needs are being adequately met?

c) What needs have you listed as number 1 priorities? What do these priority needs have in common? What is it about these needs that makes them important to you? Are they being met? Why do you think this is?
d) What needs have you listed as number 3 priorities? What do these priority needs have in common? What is it about these needs that makes them less important to you? Are your number 3 needs being met?
e) Are more or less of your number 3 needs being met as compared to your number 1 needs? Why do you think this is?

7) The second part of this exercise involves all of the needs lists you have made. Take all the lists and place a plus (+) next to each need that is being met, a slash (/) next to each need that is being partially met, and a minus (–) next to each need that is not really being met at all.

8) Place all the lists side by side and answer the following questions:

a) Whose list has the most pluses? the most slashes? the most minuses? Why do you think this is the case?
b) Whose list contains the most number 1 priorities? the most number 3 priorities? What are the reasons for this? Has this situation cahnged over the past 6 months? the past year?
c) What does this exercise tell you about how you view your own needs versus others' needs? about how you value your own needs versus others' needs? about how you meet your own needs versus others' needs?
d) Is there anything about the manner in which you meet needs that you would like to change?

9) Now take all of your lists and sit down in the middle of the floor. Start with your own list and place it in front of you.

Place the other lists in a semi-circle in front of you. As suggested earlier, you literally are surrounded by all the needs squeezing you.

10) Look at all the pages, at all the items, at all the hours, how does this make you feel?

11) Add up all the hours you have estimated would be necessary to meet everyone's needs in an average week, and answer the following questions:

a) Could any single person possibly accomplish this?
b) Do you think a person should expect to be able to meet all of these needs?
c) If you have answered *no* to *a* or *b*, ask yourself why you think you can do it.

So where are you now? In all likelihood, you now know that there are too many needs and too few hours. You knew it before because you felt it—that is probably why you are reading this book—but now you know why. Now you know why you are feeling so stressed, now you are aware of your feelings, your and their expectations, and everyone's needs. If you aren't sure about these things, loop back to the previous steps.

So where do you go from here? Save your lists and go on to the next steps of The Balancing Act.

STEP 4
Communication

What You Heard Isn't What I Said, And What I Said Isn't What I Meant

You are aware of your situation, you have a pretty good picture of the real needs and expectations that surround you, but unless you can clearly communicate this knowledge it will be of little use to you. Clear communication is the key to surviving your Big Squeeze. But it is not easy to attain.

* * * *

"I've been thinking ..." Norm Emerick said one night while having dessert with his son's family.

"Thinking about what, Dad?" his son John prompted.

"Well, you know how lonely I've been since your mother died ..." The older man swallowed hard and looked down at his hands. "Well, I just think that being in that big house all by myself is—well, it's just too big." His eyes filled with tears. "Too many memories ..."

"But Dad, I thought you loved that house?"

"I do, and I don't. Maybe it's just time to move on."

"But what about your friends? The neighbors?" John asked.

"Maybe it's just time to move on," Norm repeated.

John exchanged glances with his wife. "Where would you go? What would you do with the house?"

Norm pulled a crumpled brochure from his pocket and laid it on the table. "Retirement community. New concept, Sherm Talbot tells me." He smoothed the brochure and pointed to shiny pictures of a golf course, a large communal dining room, and tastefully-decorated apartments. "Sherm loves it there."

John looked at his wife again. "Cost a lot of money?"

Norm nodded. "I'd have to sell the house for the down payment—but my social security and savings should cover the monthly costs—as long as I don't live more than another twenty years." He looked his son straight in the eye. "You wouldn't mind, would you?"

"Of course not," John said quickly. "It's your money and your house—you should do what you want."

Norm looked at the pictures. "I guess I'm not sure what I want. But I guess it's not fair to ask you to help me decide?" He looked at his son hopefully.

John shrugged. "It's your decision, Dad. Why don't you think about it, and we'll talk about it some other time."

Norm put his fork down. "Think I'll be going now," he mumbled as he got up and left the house.

* * * *

What is going on between Norm Emerick and his son is a failure to communicate on many levels. First, Norm is not sending a clear message about his true feelings and desires, or about what he really expects from his son. In addition, John is not sending a clear message about what he really desires from his father. To make matters worse, neither father nor son is receiving the other's message.

Is it any wonder they ended the conversation frustrated and confused? Or that the problem remained unsolved?

This type of miscommunication goes on all the time, often with the same unsatisfactory result Norm and John experienced. Why? Why is it so difficult to say what we mean? And why is it so difficult to hear what is being said?

Sending errors

There are a wide variety of reasons why a person sending a message might express himself in a manner contrary to what he really feels. These reasons run the gamut from purposeful lies to the creation of confusing or contradictory messages due to unconscious feelings or motives.

For example, Norm may already know that he wants to sell the house and move to the retirement community. He may be pretending (lying) that he hasn't decided in an attempt to get his son to give him advice as a means of giving him *permission* to do exactly as he wants—because he knows John has always wanted to move *his* family to his childhood home.

Or, Norm may really want to move, but be afraid of the new situation and unconsciously afraid that moving from the house will cause him to forget—and lose contact with—his late wife. He may be unwilling to admit his fears to either himself or his son, and therefore this unconscious contradiction manifests itself in mixed messages.

Or, Norm may want his son's approval more than anything else—more than the fact that he is unable to handle the chores in the house. He knows his son wants the house, and he is offering his ambivalence as an opportunity for John to say no. Perhaps he hopes John will offer to move his family in with him.

Or perhaps, Norm equates moving to a retirement community with old age and dying—even though he pushes the thought down every time it comes to his mind—and therefore doesn't want to make this statement to the world or to himself.

These semi-conscious ambivalences can also manifest themselves in mixed messages.

Or, Norm may be crying out for help. He may be honestly confused and trying to directly solicit his son's advice; he may just be expressing himself poorly.

Receiving errors

There are almost as many reasons why a message may be misinterpreted on the receiving end. The receiving party may not be listening, may purposely misinterpret the message, may hear only what he or she wishes to hear, or perhaps, the message is so garbled that it is impossible to sort out the true meaning.

For example, John may not be tuned into his father's real ambivalence and confusion. He may retain the view of his father that he held as a child—that of a domineering and decisive man—and be completely unaware that, due to age and the loss of his wife, his father has changed. John might be completely unaware that Norm is really asking for direction.

Or, John may have his own agenda; he may be greedy and think that his father has no right to sell the house and spend *his* inheritance. Therefore, John may purposely misinterpret or avoid Norm's request in an attempt to gain his own end.

Or, perhaps John has his own agenda, but is not quite so greedy; maybe he has always longed for his father's house, always wished for his son to sleep in his old room, to play in that big back yard. Perhaps he feels he cannot be honest and open about his desires, and thinks it is necessary to pretend he is doing what is best for his father. John feels guilty about not being a good enough son, and his guilt further interferes with their communication.

Maybe John can't hear what Norm is saying because he can't admit to himself that his father is getting older. Or maybe he's completely bewildered by Norm's message. Does his father want to move, or not? Does his father want to be told what to do? Or does his father really want to decide for himself? Given Norm's unclear signals, John's perplexity may be warranted.

Erroneous assumptions

If the number of confusions involving direct sending and direct receiving weren't enough, there is another complicating factor: whether the sender and receiver thinks the message has been correctly received. For example, if Norm thinks his son has understood his need for some help in making this decision, he may be hurt and frustrated when John doesn't come to his aid with a firm recommendation. Or, if John thinks that he has correctly received his father's request to allow him to make the decision by himself, John may be hurt and confused by Norm's anger and rejection.

It's amazing that anyone ever gets the right message.

Communicating the Real Message

Covert and overt messages

The concepts of covert and overt have been discussed in relation to expectations; and it has been pointed out that, whether it is expectations or needs that are being considered, everything gets worked out through communication. Let's focus for a while on the communications themselves, on the covert and overt messages. For covert and overt messages are part of every interpersonal exchange.

As with expectations, the covert and overt messages are sometimes the same. If you are eagerly anticipating spending time with your mother, you call her and say, "I'll be there in half an hour, Mom. Looking forward to seeing you." Your voice reflects anticipation and there is no tension in the conversation; you are truly happy to be visiting her, and you are overtly and covertly expressing your true feelings.

Sometimes, the covert and overt messages are not the same at all. If you are being pulled in five different directions by your kids and your job and your broken washing machine, but your mother expects you to drop by every Friday afternoon, you call her and say, "I'll be there in half of an hour, Mom. Looking forward to seeing you." Your voice reflects frustration and tension—it is tight and cold, your words are clipped; you are annoyed and hassled because you feel obligated to visit her. Although you may be overtly expressing the *correct* sentiments, you are covertly expressing your actual sentiments. Chances are your mother will know exactly how you really feel.

Your awareness of what your covert messages are, and your ability to share your true thoughts and feelings, are the keys to clear communication. Often this awareness is difficult to achieve because the covert messages, and the reasons for them, are not easy to discover. And, particularly for normally reticent people or people who have been taught to keep their feelings to themselves, sharing may be uncomfortable and difficult to do.

Joseph Luft and Harry Ingham devised a method, called the Johari Window, for looking at both your self-awareness and your ability to share as they relate to the covert and the overt messages that are being sent. The power of the Johari Window is that it shows you how crucial both self-awareness and sharing are to achieving the goals of any communication, and how devastating the lack of awareness and sharing can be.

The Johari Window

The Johari window is a tool that uses two scales—self-awareness and sharing—to graphically depict the relative amounts of any communication that are open and direct (overt), versus those that are hidden and/or unconscious (covert). Interpretation of the Johari Window can help you understand how these two factors can affect your behavior as well as others' interpretation of that behavior.

The simplifying assumption underlying the Johari Window is that there are two important dimensions of knowledge that an individual has about a particular communication:

1) What is actually known and acknowledged by the individual;
2) What someone is willing to share with others.

A line representing the dimension of self-awareness runs across the top. A line representing what the individual is willing to share with others runs down the left-hand side. Each line is a scale from 1 to 10, with lower numbers indicating less revelation and higher numbers more revelation. The idea is that, on any given issue, your self-awareness ranges on a continuum from very little (1 or 2) to very much (9 or 10). The same is true for your willingness to share your thoughts and feelings on the subject with others. Here is an example of a Johari Window, and how it can be used to understand the covert and overt messages between Norm Emerick and his son.

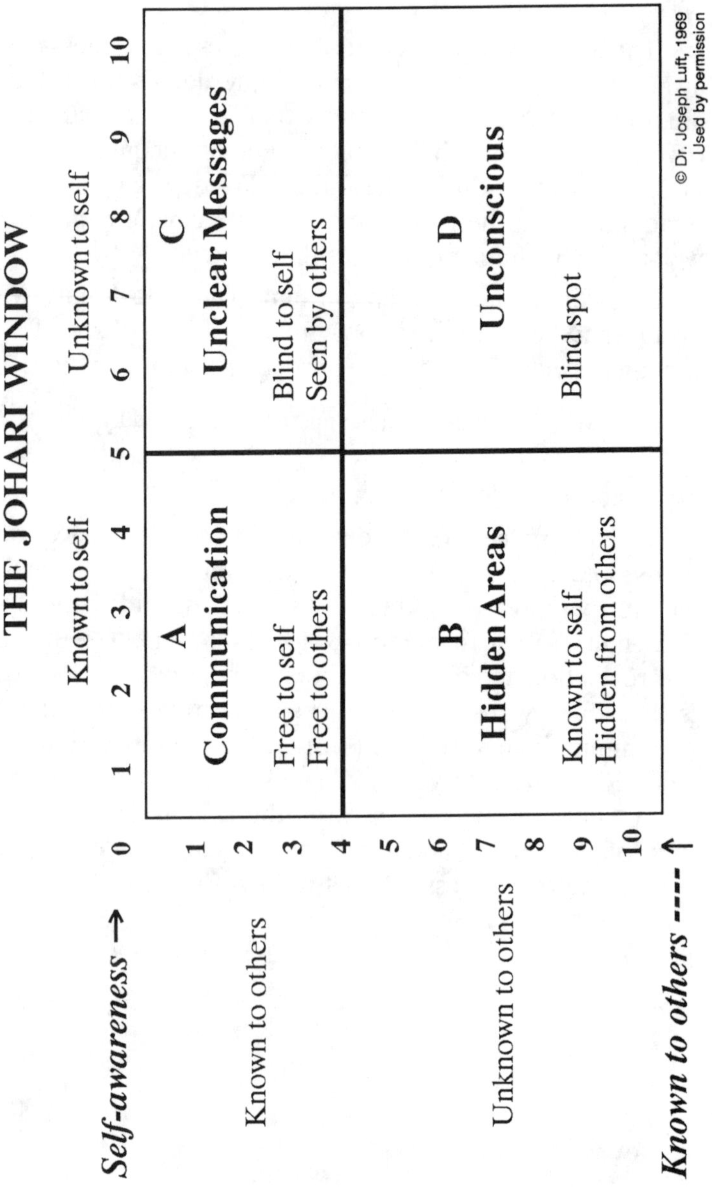
THE JOHARI WINDOW
Self-awareness →
Known to self
Unknown to self
0 1 2 3 4 5 6 7 8 9 10
Known to others
Unknown to others
A
Communication
Free to self
Free to others
C
Unclear Messages
Blind to self
Seen by others
B
Hidden Areas
Known to self
Hidden from others
D
Unconscious
Blind spot
1 2 3 4 5 6 7 8 9 10
Known to others ---- →
© Dr. Joseph Luft, 1969
Used by permission

To return to the example, perhaps Norm does want to move, but is afraid of forgetting his late wife. He knows he wants to leave the old house, but, because of his fear of even more loss, part of him doesn't want to go. He is only partially aware of the source of his ambivalence, because he only partially acknowledges his fear—most of his awareness is buried in his unconscious. Norm might score a "5" on the self-awareness line.

But what is he willing to share with others? He is willing to share his desire to move, but is unwilling (and in some ways, unable) to admit he is afraid. Norm might score a "4" on the sharing line. If a line is placed down from the "5" along the top, and another line from the "4" along the side, four boxes are formed.

The Contents of Norm Emerick's Boxes

Box A:
1) His statement that the old house is too big;
2) His statement that Sherm likes living in the retirement community.

Box B:
1) His inability to do household repair and maintenance tasks;
2) His conscious fear of losing his wife's memory;
3) His knowledge that John wants to move his family into the house.

Box C:
1) His anger at John for pressuring him into not selling the house;
2) His embarrassment over his fear of losing his wife's memory.

Box D:
1) His fear of growing old;
2) His low self-esteem due to his inability to do the things he used to do;
3) His fear of letting John down.

Box A, Communication, indicates the portion of Norm's message that is directly spoken, and obvious, to everyone. This information is free to both Norm and John; Norm knows it, and he shares it. Examples of the type of information contained in this box might be Norm's feeling that the old house is too big, and the fact that his friend Sherm likes the retirement community. As you can see from the illustration, this box is rather small; the percentage of up-front, above-board, shared information in Norm and John's interaction is about 20 percent—not very high.

Box B, Hidden Areas, contains the portion of Norm's message that he is aware of, but is unwilling to share with others; he knows it, and chooses to hide it. This box contains Norm's secrets, hopes, fears, and dreams. Examples of the type of information contained in this box might be Norm's inability to do many of the necessary maintenance and repair chores around the house, the conscious piece of his fear of losing touch with his wife's memory, and, perhaps, his knowledge that his son really wants to move into the house himself. The example shows this box to be relatively large; there is a significant piece of information that Norm is purposely withholding from the conversation—he is keeping 30 percent of this interaction hidden from his son.

Box C, Unclear Messages, contains the portion of Norm's interaction that he is blind to himself, but that may disclose itself to others; he doesn't know it, but it shows anyway. This is where hunches and intuition come from; this is how you sometimes just "get the feeling" that something other than what is being said is going on.

Examples of the type of information contained in this box might be Norm's anger at his son for pressuring him not to sell the house when that is what he really wants, his humiliation at wanting to stay in a building that makes him feel closer to a dead woman, and his embarrassment over his fear of once again losing his wife. These hidden emotions manifest themselves in his confusion and in his rejection of his son at the end of the conversation; these form the basis for many of the covert messages that Norm is sending John.

Box D, Unconscious, contains all the information in this interaction that is unavailable to any of the parties; it is buried in Norm's unconscious and is not reflected in a manner that John is aware of. It is a blind spot in the interaction and, if it forms a large piece of that interaction, can have disastrous effects.

Examples of the type of information contained in this box might be Norm's fear of growing old, his low self-esteem due to his realization that his memory and physical abilities are slipping—and his fear that because of all of these things he is letting his son down. It is irrelevant whether Norm's perceptions are true or false; because they are hidden from John, and John is unable to refute them. In this case, these unconscious, unexpressed feelings could lead to Norm's ultimate withdrawal from his son. In this example, this box is relatively large; thirty percent of this interaction is hidden to both Norm and his son.

So, what does the Johari Window tell you about Norm and John's conversation? It shows that only a small fragment of the important information about the situation is overt and known by both parties, and that the majority of the underlying knowledge and feelings are covert and unavailable to either Norm or John—or to both.

It is likely that a conversation in which approximately 80 percent of the relevant feelings and thoughts are hidden from at least one of the participants has a good chance of being misunderstood. Therefore, this Johari Window indicates that confusion, misreading, mistakes, and possibly bad feelings are a probable result for Norm and his son.

So, what can be done? The answer—for Norm and for you—is to make Box A, the overt portion of the communication, as large as possible; you also need to acknowledge that the areas you choose to keep hidden will most likely communicate themselves anyway. Increasing the overt portion of your message can be accomplished in two ways: by being more self-aware and honest with yourself, and by choosing to be more open and forthright with others.

To return to the example, if Norm were more honest about his true feelings, he would be more aware of both his fear of losing his wife's memory, and of his desire for freedom from the maintenance and repair chores. Acknowledgement of these feelings might allow him to see that these are valid feelings, and thereby allow him to express them more directly to his son. This would decrease the amount of information he is purposely withholding in the conversation. In terms of the Johari Window, Norm's self-awareness and sharing scores might both move up to "7." If you draw lines for these numbers, you will see that Box A has been greatly increased; it now encompasses roughly two-thirds of the communication.

What does this mean for the interaction? With Norm being more honest and direct with his son, John can respond to the real message—rather than to a convoluted one. John can now see where his father's ambivalence derives, and he will be better equipped to respond appropriately. If you made a Johari Window for John, increasing his awareness of his desire to live in his father's house would also have a strong positive impact on their conversation.

This same strategy can work for you. *Communication Exercise I*, will help you diagram your own Johari Window, in order to determine how self-aware you think you are, and how much sharing you believe you are willing to do. The importance of this cannot be overestimated: while you have no control over other's ability to hear you, you do have control over how clear and direct your messages are.

Communication Exercise I

1) Ask yourself the following question: How much of your own feelings toward your parent(s) are you in touch with? Think about it for a while—it's a complicated question. Then, using a copy of the Johari Window diagram, place a mark on the number along the top of the square that corresponds to

your degree of your true self-awareness in relation to your parent(s). A score of 1 indicates that you are not at all aware of the web of emotions, underlying issues or motives that drive your relationship with your parent(s). A score of 10 indicates that you believe you are aware of *all* of these issues.

2) Ask yourself how much you are willing to share what you know about your thoughts and feelings regarding your parent(s). Again, this is also a very complicated question. After you have thought about it for a while, place a mark on the number along the left-hand side of the square that corresponds to the degree you are willing to disclose your true feelings to your parent(s). A score of 1 indicates that you are not at all willing to share anything that you feel with them. A score of 10 indicates that you believe you share everything you feel and think about them and your relationship with them.

3) Starting at the marks you have made on the two dimensions, draw the lines that will divide the Johari Window into four boxes.

4) Look at the four boxes and ask yourself the following questions:

a) Which ones are the smallest, the largest? Why do you think this is?
b) How big is Box A? Is this the way you want it to be?
c) If Box A is not the way you want it to be:
   1. Why are you hiding so much of yourself, from yourself, and from your parent(s)?
   2. What does it do for you?
   3. How does it affect them?
   4. What stops you from trusting your parent(s) enough to talk about your true thoughts and feelings?
   5. Have you always had that type of relationship?
   6. Is this the way you want it to continue?
   7. How would you feel if this is how your children felt about, and treated, you?

8. What steps might you take to increase your self-awareness?
9. What steps might you take to increase your ability to share your true feelings with your parent(s)?

d) Everything below the horizontal line is hidden and unspoken to your parents.

1. Is this how you want it to be?
2. If not, why do you think it is so?
3. If you aren't sure, loop back to awareness.

e) Everything to the right of the vertical line is hidden to you.

1. Is this how you want it?
2. If not, why do you think it is so?
3. How much do you think your lack of awareness is impacting your life?

The benefits of this exercise are three-fold:

1) It should make you more aware of your directness (or lack thereof) and honesty (or lack thereof) with both yourself and others;

2) It should help you begin to see how important these two dimensions are—and how much a small change in either one can affect the clarity of your communication;

3) It should give you some clues as to where you can begin to implement positive change.

* * * *

Communication Exercise II, your parents' Johari Window, will help you see the picture from the other side: how self-aware and sharing your parents are. Analysis of these two exercises will help you move more of your motives and feelings into awareness, and aid you in seeing the motives and feelings that underlie your parents' communication. This should enable you to act by choice rather than impulse in all levels of communication with your parents, and enable them to react to your real, rather than your hidden, messages.

Here, the interest is in communication from your parents' point of view. Obviously, you can't be as aware of their true feelings as you can be of your own—but you can make guesses and perhaps explore some hunches about what is really going on between you and your parents. And hopefully, improve your communications with them.

Communication Exercise II

1) How much of your parents' feelings about their relationship with you are they in touch with? Think about it for a while—it's a complicated question from this perspective, too. Then, using a fresh copy of the diagram, place a mark on the number along the top of the square that corresponds to your estimate of their degree of true self-awareness in relation to you. A score of 1 indicates that they are not at all aware of the web of emotions, underlying issues, or motives that drive your relationship. A score of 10 indicates that you believe they are aware of *all* of these issues.

2) How much of what they know about their thoughts and feelings regarding your relationship are they willing to share with you? Again, this is also a very complicated question. After you have thought about it for a while, place a mark on the number along the left-hand side of the square that corresponds to the degree they are willing to disclose their true feelings to you. A score of 1 indicates that they are not at all willing to share anything that they feel with you. A score of 10 indicates that they share everything that they feel and think about you and about your relationship.

3) Starting at the marks you have made on the two dimensions, draw the lines that will divide the Johari Window into four boxes.

4) Look at the four boxes and ask yourself the following questions:

a) Which are the smallest, the largest? Why do you think this is?
b) How big is Box A? Is this the way you want it to be? Is it the way *they* want it to be?
c) If Box A is not the way you want it to be:
   1) Why are they hiding so much of themselves —from themselves and from you?
   2) What does it do for them?
   3) How does it affect you?
   4) What stops them from trusting you enough to talk about their true thoughts and feelings?
   5) Have you always had this kind of relationship?
   6) Is this the way you want it to continue?
   7) How aware do you think they are of their lack of honesty with themselves and you?
   8) What steps might you take to increase their self-awareness?
   9) What steps might you take to increase their ability to share their true feelings with you?
   10) If there is nothing you can do to change them, is there anything you can do that might make Box A larger?

Obviously, your ability to affect a change in your parents' self-awareness and level of sharing is much more limited than your ability to affect your own. But there are ways you can have an impact. You can talk to them directly about these issues. You can subtly probe and suggest ways that might make them—and you—more aware of their lack of openness. And you all might look at the answers. Why are things the way they are? Why is it that your parents are more open with your sister than they are with you?

Perhaps you will discover that their lack of openness is affected by your lack of willingness to hear them. For example, how open are you to talking to them about what they want done after they die? Often it is the adult child, rather than the older adult, who is leery of the topic of death. What do you do when your parents want to discuss their will? or their funeral? or who should get the diamond ring? Perhaps they are more open with your sister because she is more open to them.

On the other hand, sometimes there is nothing you can do that will directly change how open they are with themselves or with you—perhaps the only thing you can do is use your increased insight to improve the communication as much as possible. Increased insight can be a powerful tool.

Awareness of the power of these two dimensions, and awareness of communication patterns in general, can greatly improve your ability to express yourself effectively to all the significant people in your life. If your messages are based on a strong understanding of yourself (loop back to Step 1 if necessary), they can have a powerful and positive impact on how everyone perceives the expectations (loop back to Step 2) and needs (loop back to Step 3) involved in the situation.

This is not to say that everyone will be happy; there still may be conflict, but it will be based on honest and open expression of feelings. These feelings can then be discussed and explored—rather than seething unrecognized below the surface of your relationships.

Communication is the cornerstone of any relationship. Honesty and openness are the key to effective communication.

STEP 5
Resources

Peg Clancy stopped at a red light and began mentally running down her to-do-list for the afternoon: food shop for Mom—done; set up skating lessons for Robin—done; order birthday cake for Dan—done; pick up PTA flyers from Marge—done; bring food to Mom—on the way; cook dinner for Mom—still to do; pick up David at soccer practice—still to do; get her own family's dinner ready—still to do, still to do, still to do .... Peg sighed. It always seemed like there was so much still to do. If only her sister Martha were available to help more with Mom, but unfortunately she lived half-way across the country.

* * * *

When Ed Tirrel finally got home it was after 8:00 p.m.; he was exhausted, his dinner was cold, and his wife was furious. Just as Ed had been leaving work, his father had called in a panic because the toilet in his apartment had overflowed and he was unable to reach the superintendent. Ed promised to stop by and take a quick look at the problem — unfortunately, it hadn't been quite as easy to solve as he had thought it would be.

* * * *

Faith Enos' mother had lost her husband the previous spring, her best friend last month, and two of her canasta-club cronies during the past year; the older woman was sad, lonely and depressed—and on the phone to her daughter at least three times a day. Faith wanted to be there for her mother, she understood that her mother needed contact and interaction, that her mother needed love and reassurance. But the time and energy it all demanded, as well as the emotional stamina necessary, was wearing her out—and not leaving her any time for her job or her husband or her kids. Her brother lived two thousand miles away—a call far too costly for her mother to make more than a couple of times a month.

* * * *

Peg, Ed, and Faith are all "good" adult children, responding freely and helpfully to the needs of their elderly parents. But are they really helping their parents, if, as a result of trying to meet their parents' needs, they are denying their own needs and the needs of their families? And even if they are still helping their parents, what is the cost? And is the cost too great to pay?

Is it ever possible to meet everyone's needs without overstressing yourself, denying someone, or perhaps alienating someone else? In some situations the answer is probably *no*; in others, the answer may be *yes*. But often, in attempting to meet one person's needs you are—almost by definition—not meeting the needs of someone else's.

For example, in your attempt to help your mother deal with the death of your father, you began inviting her to spend Friday nights with your family. You and your husband were happy to help her, and didn't mind giving up your time together because you had Saturday nights to spend as a couple. But after breaking up with her boyfriend, your daughter has been having a difficult time and has joined you for a movie and dinner for the last six Saturday nights. Now your relationship with your husband is suffering. How can you be a "good" daughter, a "good" mother, and a "good" wife all at the same time? Is it ever possible? Or are they mutually exclusive?

It will never be possible if you try to do it alone; it will never be possible until you accept the idea of interdependence. It will never be possible until you open your eyes to all the other sources of help that surround you: your siblings, your spouse, your children, your parents—and a wide variety of community resources.

Perhaps the solution to the good daughter-mother-wife problem is right before your eyes: perhaps your daughter and mother would enjoy spending Saturday nights together. This would allow you and your husband to have your alone time, while providing the companionship both the older and younger women need. A perfect—but unfortunately rare—solution.

Sometimes the solutions are fairly simple. Most times they are not. But the good news is that there is probably a lot more help out there than you think.

Your Support Network

You developed an awareness during step one that you were surrounded by a large web of relationships, and you saw that each person or organization in this web was a potential source of both demand and support. Unfortunately, you are probably more used to thinking about each of them in terms of the demands they place on you; now it is time to turn that perception around and look at each person or organization as a potential source of support.

If Peg Clancy did this she might discover that although her sister Martha was unable to help out on a daily basis, Martha might be more than happy to send money to pay for a *Meals On Wheels* food delivery service for their mother. Ed Tirrel might learn that his son Gregory, who adores his grandfather, would be more than happy to stop by after school a couple of times a week—and perhaps lend a hand with any chores that might need doing. And Faith Enos might find out that her brother's company's benefit package offers money toward adult day care for employees with elderly parents, or that there is a weekly bereavement group at her mother's church, or that Medicare would pay for some short-term counselling to help the older woman with her lingering depression.

You too may find that there are many members of your own network who are able—and even willing—to help, perhaps in ways you hadn't considered before. Often, the people who have the greatest potential to support you are the ones you perceive to put the most demands on you. Your mother may be able to cook her own meals, if she could just get to the store. Your daughter may be able to arrange a car pool for her part-time job. Your husband can take his own suits to the cleaners. And you may find your company is willing to give you time off to search for a nursing home. *Resource Exercise I* will help you determine the strengths of those within your network.

Resource Exercise I

1) In *Needs Exercise I* you compiled a list of your main characters (derived from the first three columns of your *Awareness Exercise I* list) and your supporting cast (derived from the first list of your *Awareness Exercise II*). As you did in *Needs Exercise I,* place the name of each person or organization on the top of a separate sheet of paper. This stack of paper comprises your immediate support network.

2) On each person or organization's piece of paper, list their abilities, hobbies, characteristics, areas of interest, positive personality traits, and any other pieces of information you think might be relevant to their ability to support anyone—not just you.

a) Your list for your Aunt Sally might include: (1) good cook, (2) likes to sew, (3) likes to read, (4) likes children, (5) plays bridge, (6) likes to talk, (7) cheerful, (8) has a car.
b) Your list for your sister Julia might include: (1) financial planner, (2) skier, (3) good with her hands, (4) makes a lot of money, (5) close to Dad while growing up, (6) good sense of humor, (7) has a car.
c) Your list for your company might include: (1) cafeteria-style benefit package including day care, health club, and/or dental coverage, (2) computers, (3) Xerox and fax machines, (4) flex-time.
d) Don't worry about whether your lists reflect anyone's ability to meet actual needs—just make the lists and save them.

Their Support Networks

The same way you are surrounded by a network of people and organizations, so too is each one of your *main characters.* Their networks are a source of support for them, and also for you—although it is dangerous to assume that these secondary and tertiary levels of support will be there for you on a regular basis. It is probably most useful for you to consider them as sources of emergency support, as a safety net you might not be able to count on day-to-day—but a net that is there to catch you during those times you are the most overwhelmed.

If Peg Clancy looked into it, she might find that on a day she was particularly harried, Robin's friend Nan's mother would be more than happy to sign Robin up for skating—she was going to be there signing Nan up anyway. Ed Tirrel might suggest to his father that he ask his neighbor Nathan—who used to be a plumber—for advice about the toilet next time. And Faith Enos might discover that the woman who lives in the apartment next to her mother had also recently lost her husband—and was lonely and looking for companionship.

Resource Exercise II will help you determine the strengths of those in the networks besides yourself. Again, these are not avenues of support that you can depend on the same way you can depend on your family or on community resources—but they are sources of support nonetheless.

Resource Exercise II

1) In *Awareness Exercise II* you made up a list of the ten persons and institutions each of your main characters came into contact with on a weekly basis. Get that list and put the name of each person or institution on the top of a piece of paper. This stack of papers comprises their support networks.

2) As in *Resource Exercise I,* on each person or organization's piece of paper, list their abilities, hobbies, characteristics, areas of interest, positive personality traits, and any other pieces of information you think might be relevant to their ability to support anyone—not just the person whose network they are in. You may need assistance from the person whose network you are assessing.

a) Your father's friend Jerry's list might include: (1) likes to play poker, (2) likes to eat, (3) has a good sense of humor, (4) has a car.
b) Your mother's church list might include: (1) biweekly senior activities, (2) Sunday services, (3) Friday night pot-luck dinners, (4) bereavement groups, (5) counseling services.
c) Your daughter's friend Nina's list might include: (1) likes to skate, (2) has a mother who is very active in high school activities, (3) has many slumber parties, (4) has her own car.
d) Once again, don't worry about whether the lists reflect anyone's ability to meet an actual need—just make the lists and save them.

Community Support Networks

As the elderly population grows, so too does the number and range of community services to provide for the needs of the elderly and their families. There is a National Association of Area Agencies on Aging (NAAA) which plans and oversees many types of community-based service programs; currently, they have on-going programs in every state. Many of these services are subsidized and supplied to the client free of cost, or available on a sliding-fee scale; others may be covered by Medicaid, also known as Title XIX.

In addition, almost every community offers a wide range of medical, psychological, social, in-home and residential options for the elderly and their families. These too may be offered free of cost or on a sliding-fee scale.

The issue of cost is always a relevant one when determining the particular services appropriate for your family. While specific financial aid or government monies (Title XIX) may be available—and you are encouraged to get as much information as possible on all your parent is entitled to—there are other aspects of your financial situation it might be useful to consider.

For example, ask yourself the following questions. What makes more sense, for your parent to leave you money in their will, or for them to spend it to make their—and your—life easier? What makes more sense, for you to take the family for that expensive ski weekend, or for you to spend the money to replace yourself as your mother's housekeeper for the next year? What makes more sense, for your father to continue to subsidize your daughter's summer camp, or for him to spend the money on a chore service to help him around his house?

This is not to say these are easy decisions, but there may be more *choice* involved in financial decisions than you think. Neither choice may appeal to you, but they are still choices.

It is beyond the scope of this book to list the agencies and services available in every community, instead this section will describe the types of services that can be found within most communities. For information specific to your locale, contact the U.S. Administration on Aging or look in the yellow pages for your local Area Agency on Aging.

One way to think about the types of available services is to visualize a line ranging from activities and preventative programs for the well elderly, to institutional care for those who are unable to manage for themselves; services for the temporarily ill and the frail elderly living at home would fall in the middle of this continuum.

It may come as a surprise to you to learn that the majority of the elderly (four out of every five) live in the community; only 5 percent of those over 65 reside in a nursing home on any given day. This would be impossible for them—and for their families—without these broad-based community support systems.

These programs are there to help your parent—and taking advantage of them will most likely help you find some balance in your life. But, as with most aspects of your Big Squeeze, deciding which services to use is not a job you can do on your own. You are talking about your parent's life—how they will spend their days, and perhaps their money—therefore, it is their interests that are paramount. Wherever and whenever possible, your role should be one of support; **your job is to help your parents choose the services that they want for themselves—not to select the options for them.**

Commissions and organizations

There are both national and local organizations and commissions whose primary concerns are advocacy and assistance to the elderly. Most can be found through listings in your yellow pages.

American Association of Retired Persons (AARP). This is a non-profit organization whose membership is open to all those over 50 years of age. This group works on the national level to influence legislation beneficial to the elderly, and local chapters provide information and activities (monthly trips, speakers, programs, etc.) of special interest to older adults. AARP also provides information and discounts on drugs, medical equipment, optical wear, and insurance programs with a special low-price, mail-order pharmacy available to members.

Local Commission on Aging. Your local commission acts as a liaison between the older community and the particular town or city in which your parent lives. Their primary function is as a referral source for local services.

Local Commission on the Handicapped. Your local commission serves essentially the same function to the handicapped community that your Local Commission on Aging serves for the older community: as a referral for local handicapped services.

Area Coalition on Aging. Many communities have these groups. They are comprised of older adults as well as professionals and organizations who serve the elderly. The purpose of these coalitions is to provide advocacy and education for older adults, with primary concern focusing on ways to improve the quality of life for all elders—especially those with low incomes.

Commission for the Deaf and Hearing Impaired. These programs are generally state-run and focus on providing educational materials to the community, as well as vocational assistance to the deaf. Often special loans and grants are administered through these programs.

Mental Health and Counseling Services

Almost all communities have counseling services with the explicit purpose of helping individuals and families with any number of problems: aging, intergenerational and adolescent problems, sandwich generation issues, and overall stress management. Concrete services, assessment services, and consultation services are all generally provided by these agencies. They can be found in your yellow pages under such headings as: Jewish Family Services, Catholic Family Services, Child and Family Service, Mental Health Clinics, Child Guidance Clinics, and Outpatient Units of local hospitals.

Access services

Coordinated by your Area Agency on Aging, access services can assist you and your parent in determining your needs, and what resources are available and appropriate to service them. These services often include an assessment of your particular situation, development of a service or treatment plan, referrals, and sometimes transportation.

Many kinds of examinations and screenings (from routine health to pre-nursing home) may be performed, and information on the specifics of your situation (from your family's finances to your parent's daily activities) are often collected. Based on this information, you and your parent will be told of the appropriate public and private services available to you. Transportation and contacts with the agencies are often provided.

Community-based services

Within most communities there are a number of direct services available to all residents. The costs for these services vary by community and income level of the individual, but there are often a variety of ways that monetary obstacles can be overcome. Even if you think that you or your parent can not afford a particular program, it is worth investigating the options; financial subsidies may be available.

The following is a partial listing of the common types of community-based programs and services for the elderly. For specific information on what is available in your city or town, call your town social service department or your family service agency.

Adult day care. These programs provide support, supervision, and social activities appropriate for the functional level of the older adult, within a safe and protected setting. Adult day care is organized around a group, provided outside the home, and attended according to a pre-planned schedule.

Programs vary, but most offer social, artistic, educational, and cultural activities as well as meals, personal care and, transportation. The settings also vary; they range from small, home-style situations to larger, more school-like surroundings; some specialize in services for the highly-functional, while others support the needs of those requiring more medical care or supervision. In either case, adult day care can be a great solution for a lonely or bored elder.

Congregate meals. Often hot meals are available on a regular basis at senior centers, schools, housing complexes, churches, and synagogues. These programs are overseen by the local Area Agency on Aging to ensure that minimum daily nutritional standards are met, and can provide well-balanced, hot meals for your parent without you, or they, having to spend hours shopping and cooking. When combined with community-based transportation programs, congregate meals can give your parent both independence, companionship, and a change of scene that helps break up the day.

Legal assistance. Unfortunately, there are many difficult and complex legal problems that you and your parent may be facing: power of attorney, guardianship, wills, age discrimination, etc. Many communities offer legal services to help you with these issues.

Usually these advocacy and legal services are provided on a sliding scale by persons concerned with protecting the rights and property of your parent, and providing advice and counsel to all of you. For further information call your local bar association, legal aid (in the yellow pages), local family service agency, or town social service department.

Senior center programs. Senior centers are proliferating across the country; there are currently over 12,000 centers providing all kinds of activities—social, physical, religious, cultural, and recreational—to hundreds of thousands of elderly. Your local senior center can be a wonderful place for your parent to spend time and develop friendships and new interests, while allowing you the space you need to take care of yourself and the other obligations in your life. You will find these listed in the yellow pages of your telephone book.

Transportation services. Many communities have local transportation services featuring wheelchair-accessible vehicles specifically designed to meet the needs of elderly and disabled persons. These systems typically operate on a demand-responsive (users call ahead of time), door-to-door basis. Some towns also operate intra-community, fixed-route services that are often handicapped-accessible and may meet the needs of the elderly. Finally, some senior centers and other programs may provide their own transportation services. For example, the Red Cross often offers transportation to doctors' offices, and your local cancer society may provide assistance in getting to cancer-treatment related appointments.

The costs for these services vary, but they are often subsidized by the town, the state, or a social service agency. Some town-run transportation systems offer a sliding-scale fee for a specific number of trips per month. Sometimes there is a set cost per run, and sometimes a voluntary donation is requested. Some planning is usually involved in using these systems, for it is often necessary to call ahead to arrange for pick-up or to find out the specifics of the routes.

Long-distance elder care programs. This is a fairly new concept, found in a few metropolitan areas with large elderly populations. These programs are designed for the adult child who lives too far from his or her parent to be able to ensure that the parent is getting the correct, and the best, services available. These programs are typically run out of social service or private agencies, and will assess your parent's needs, match those needs with the available services, and then orchestrate the provision of the needed services. The adult child—not the elderly parent—is the client.

Although the costs may initially seem quite high (they are usually determined on a sliding scale relative to the adult child's income), they may not be as prohibitive as you think—for they may cost a lot less than flying across the country every month to check-in on your mother.

Employment services. If your parent is healthy and employable, you may find that your local community has specially-designed programs to help him or her find a job. These services can range from testing and counseling to resume writing and job placement. Having a job has a myriad of positive results: from feeling productive and increasing self-esteem, to partial or total financial independence. Look in the yellow pages under Job Bank, or call your town's social service agency, Area Agency on Aging, or family service center for more information.

Educational services. There are many educational services available in most communities. Sometimes these are specific programs geared to the interests of the elderly run out of the local high school, senior center, churches, or synagogues. In addition, older students are often welcomed and encouraged —some places even offer elder discounts—at many community colleges and universities. Elderhostels—offering inexpensive, short-term academic programs at educational institutions around the world—are sensational opportunities available to senior citizens. If cost is a factor, elderhostel sometimes offers needy elders "hostelships" at nearby institutions, at greatly reduced fees.

Support groups. This concept—a group of people dealing with a similar problem meeting to share their experiences and concerns—has grown in popularity in all segments of society. In most communities you will find a number of ongoing support groups that may be of assistance to both you and your parent. Often churches, synagogues, senior centers, mental health clinics, and family service agencies run support groups focusing on issues of grieving, aging, and other family problems (including sandwich generation concerns). Many other organizations run groups focusing on the issues facing their specific area of concern: The American Diabetes Association, Cancer Society, American Heart Association, Arthritis Association, Red Cross, Alzheimer's Association, etc. Use your yellow pages to find the agency that is most likely to be able to help you with your specific problems.

Financial aid. Help with financial problems is also available in most communities. On the national level, the Veterans Administration and the Social Security Administration can often be valuable sources of information. Information about services and eligibility for programs within your state can be found through your state Department of Human Resources and Department of Income Maintenance. Here is a list of state and federal subsidy programs for which you or your parent may be eligable. You can get more information on these services and programs by calling the offices listed.

Federal and State Financial Subsidy Programs

Department on Aging
- Clearing House for Elder Services
- Elder Abuse and Neglect Services
- Prescription Drug Assistance

Department of Human Resources
- Food Stamps
- Surplus Commodities Program

Department of Housing and Urban Development (HUD)
Department of Income Maintenance
- General Assistance
- State Supplement for the Aged, Blind or Disabled
- Medicaide

Social Security Office (800-234-5772)
- Old Age, Survivors and Disability In surance (OASDI)
- Medicare (800-262-4414)
- Legal Assistance to Medicare Patients (LAMP)
- Supplemental Security Income

U.S. Department of Veteran Affairs
- Educational Assistance
- Disability Compensation
- Vocational Rehabilitation
- Medical Care
- Life Insurance
- Burial Benefits

Many towns have social service divisions that can give you information on the types of locally available assistance, often including energy assistance programs, tax-abatement programs, and reverse annuity mortgage programs.

There are a wide variety of financial assistance programs for housing on the federal, state, and local levels. These usually involve some sort of government subsidization of rent payments (Section 8 Housing Assistance Payment Program), but sometimes also include government payment of up to 60 percent of both rent and utilities. Call your local Housing Authority, Department on Housing (DOH), Department of Housing and Urban Development (HUD), or town social services department to find out what is available in your area, and if your parent qualifies for assistance.

Local hospitals. This is an often-overlooked souce of support, available in almost all communities. Most hospitals have a home care and services department, a social service department, a lifeline, senior citizen health clinics, and outpatient mental health services. Call your hospital for details.

Library and reading services. Your community library is a great source of entertainment and programs for all ages, but libraries may also have programs geared to the specific needs of the elderly. Bookmobiles may be available to bring reading materials to the home-bound. Talking Book tapes may be available for the sight-impaired, and in some communities there may even be a Blind and Physically Handicapped Department within the local library.

In-home services

Another set of community programs that can be of tremendous aid to you and your parent are in-home services designed to allow the elderly to stay independent, and living at home, for as long as possible. You may be surprised to discover that many of the things you spend hours doing can be provided to your parent by others—often at a lower cost than you might expect. These services—homemakers, companions, cooks, cleaning people, drivers, handymen—can free you from the time-consuming practical side of your parent's care, and leave you more available to meet your parent's emotional needs—and perhaps even enhance the mutual enjoyment in your relationship.

Home-delivered meals. One of the most useful services available to those who cannot shop and cook for themselves are programs that deliver meals directly to the home; in many communities these programs are called Meals-On-Wheels. The beauty of this type of service is that it can keep your parent independent, functioning, and out of a nursing home—and keep you sane, and available for more important things.

Although this may appear expensive at first glance, the cost is not as great as you might think once you take the price of the food into consideration. Home-delivered meals also compare very favorably to nursing-home costs, and may offer a way for a financially-established, out-of-town sibling to contribute.

Homemaker services. Again, this is a potentially expensive option for the parent who is unable to do his own housekeeping, but you may find that in some instances this service is covered through Title XIX. And it can be a real time and sanity saver for you. It can also be used intermittently, on a fee-for-service basis. Usually homemaker services include shopping, light housecleaning, meal preparation, and laundry. Again, this is a much less expensive option than nursing-home care.

Chore services. An invaluable, but also potentially expensive, way to help your parent with home maintenance chores, these services range from heavier cleaning (floors and windows) to yard work and minor home repairs. As with homemaker services, they are available on an as-needed basis, and can also be a way for the out-of-town relative to contribute.

Home-health services. Unlike homemaker and chore services, home-health services may be covered by insurance or entitlement programs like Title XIX. They are usually carried out under a nurse's or doctor's supervision, and run the gamut from physical therapy, to medication and shots, to teaching family members about ongoing care. Services may include hands-on help with bathing, personal care, ambulatory assistance, and homemaker support.

Up until very recently, local Departments of Human Resources, Income Maintenance and Aging helped pay for home health aides. However, due to the fiscal situation as of this writing—June 1991—many of these agencies have either reduced or eliminated this assistance. Call any of these agencies to get current information on what is available in your state.

Generally, if your parent has just been released from the hospital (and is therefore covered by Medicare) or has a High Option Health Care Policy (that covers home health services) it is only necessary to call a licensed, bonded Home Health Care Service. The service will send someone out to the home or the hospital, make an assessment, contact Medicare or the private insurer, and develop a plan which includes payment issues and schedules. It is important to note that Medicare only pays for designated amounts of skilled nursing care generally provided by a certified home health aide who is periodically supervised by a registered nurse.

Medicaid (Title XIX) coverage for a home health aide for parents with very low incomes. Qualification guidelines differ from state to state, but generally an individual's assets can not exceed a few thousand dollars, and monthly income must be low as well.

Unfortunately, if your parent is above the income eligibility guidelines or is not covered by either Medicare or private insurance, they will have to cover this expense themselves. There are basically only two options available in this situation: (1) pay the home health care service costs yourself, or (2) arrange for a lower-cost, unbonded, unlicensed homemaker described above.

Telephone reassurance. These programs are usually staffed by volunteers, and are often free of charge. Usually, volunteers call your parent on a regular basis (once a week); these calls ensure that your parent is safe, as well as give him or her someone to talk to—thereby decreasing their social isolation, loneliness,and dependence on you. Check your yellow pages or with your social service agency to find out if this is available in your community.

Friendly visiting. These programs are similar to telephone-reassurance programs in that they are usually carried out by volunteers—making them free of charge—for the purpose of decreasing the social isolation of the home-bound. You can arrange for someone to periodically stop by and visit your parent, providing regular companionship and someone to talk to besides you. Unfortunately, volunteerism—especially among those with access to a car—is on the decline, and there are often waiting lists for these services.

Energy assistance and weatherization. Most states offer some type of low-income energy and weatherization assistance. This varies from help paying fuel bills to the installation of storm windows and insulation. Call your town social service agency or your power company for information.

Emergency-response systems. A wide variety of emergency-response systems have come on the market in recent years. They may be costly direct hook-ups with hospitals or police, or less costly cellular systems. These systems can help the elderly stay independent, while reassuring you—and them—that help will be available in times of emergency.

It is advisable to do some investigation of these services, for they vary widely in both quality, price, and features. Some are voice-activated, while others require that a button be pushed; some have high up-front costs for expensive equipment, while others are paid for by a monthly fee.

Respite care. Although this service is not available in all communities—and prices vary based on the type of service—it can be extremely helpful if you are actively caring for your parent. Respite care allows you to take a break by approving someone to come in and take over care-giving responsibilities for a short time. This is sometimes available through social service agencies (i.e. United Way, Cerebral Palsy, etc.) or home-health agencies.

Residential subsidies

Housing subsidy programs vary in both type and eligibility, but most of them are only available to older adults with low incomes; the requirements differ from state to state and project to project. Call you local Department of Housing, Town Housing Authority or Department on Aging for the specifics for your locale.

Subsidized housing for the low-income elderly. These housing situations are typically clusters of apartments providing housing for low-income seniors who are on social security (income maximums are usually around $15,000 for individuals and $18,500 for couples). The total rent paid by the older adult is usually about 30 percent of their income (often after medical expenses are subtracted), with the balance of the rent subsidized by the federal government, usually through Section 8.

Services within these communities vary widely: some offer community rooms and hot meals, others provide no services. Presently, very few complexes of this type are being built, and there are often long waiting lists for those that do exist. If you think this might be appropriate for your parent, it would make sense to look into potential locations at least a year of two before you think it might be needed.

Conventional apartments with subsidies. In many areas it is possible to get a Section 8 Subsidy Certificate for a conventional apartment—assuming both your parent and the apartment meet the criteria. Your parent must meet the maximum income requirements, and the apartment must meet certain size and price standards; the landlord must also be willing to go through the paperwork and inspections necessary to be approved for this program.

Homeshare programs. Many communities have homeshare programs through local family service agencies in which a group of older adults share a house or apartment. Interested parties register with the programs and are interviewed for appropriate matches. Unfortunately, these programs are not widespread and are limited in scope, but they have been very successful in some situations. For information on the availability of this type of program in your community, call your local family service agency, town social service department, or the Area Agency on Aging.

Residential communities

There may come a time when your parent does not desire, or is unable, to continue to live at home. For those who do not require extensive medical care, and for those for whom living with a child or a relative is not desired or appropriate, there is a continuum of retirement-community options available.

Retirement communities are usually appropriate for those who are basically healthy, independent, and not under severe financial constraints—although there is a wide variation in type, services, and costs. Some communities have no medical facilities; others are associated with nursing homes. Some require the purchase of a condominium or cooperative unit; others are rentals with no down payment necessary; and in yet others, the costs may be reimbursed for low-income elders qualifying for Section 8 housing assistance. Some assume complete autonomy of the residents; others provide two to three meals a day.

Independent living. These communities are at the minimum-support end of the retirement community spectrum. Typically, these are complexes (some rental and some condominium) with laundry, meals, and recreation available under one roof—frequently there is a recreational director on-site who orchestrates events for the residents, and often transportation services are provided. Although a meal or two is generally served at the communal dining hall, and daily or weekly housekeeping is often available, the assumption is that the older adults wish to live independent lives.

Assisted living. These communities provide the mid-range of support. Usually three meals a day are provided, and health aides are available to assist residents in all areas of personal care: dressing, bathing, etc. But the older adults still have their own apartments and live moderately independent lives.

Home health aides and homemakers are also available throughout the day for additional assistance, although it is assumed that a constant companion is not necessary. If more care is needed, the community will often assist you in finding someone. These communities have all the amenities of Independent Living Communities, while also having the additional personnel necessary to handle the needs of individual residents. The costs are correspondingly higher.

Life care. Here, while still providing semi-independent living opportunities, communities are usually associated with nursing homes—some even have nursing homes on the grounds. The residents of these communities are generally less independent—or perhaps one spouse is less independent. Life Care Communities provide a living option for those not sick enough to require a nursing home, but not well enough to be truly independent.

The assumption is that your parent can move into the community and remain there for the rest of his or her life. These communities usually include all the aspects of Independent Living and Assisted Living Communities—with the addition of a convalescent home on-site.

These communities are generally quite expensive, but prices and payment options vary widely. In some instances, your mother might buy a home and live in it for the duration of her life, but it would revert back to the community upon her death. In other cases, the home is an asset of her estate, although it may decrease in value by a given percentage each year.

Institutional facilities

Institutional facilities are for those who, while not needing the intensive care offered in a hospital, are not really able to care for themselves. In the past, nursing homes were seen only as long-term facilities, but this need not be the case; they may be a viable option if, for example, your parent has just been released from the hospital or is recovering from a short-term disability. Or they may be a long-term solution for a physically or mentally-disabled parent.

Skilled nursing facilities/intermediate care facilities. Up until 1991, skilled nursing facilities and intermediate care facilities were offered as separate services—skilled facilities provided care to the seriously ill on a 24-hour basis, and intermediate facilities cared for those who were less seriously ill. These two types are now combined; any certified nursing home is able to care for either type of patient. Specialized services are often offered (rehabilitative, Alzheimer's units, etc.) and those that are federally certified are covered by Medicare and Medicaid programs.

Board and care facilities. These facilities offer room, board, and care without medical or skilled nursing services, and are appropriate for those who can not live alone, but are not seriously ill. This type of facility is not usually licensed to receive reimbursement under Medicare or Medicaid, and they can be prohibitively expensive. In some states, however, residents may be eligible for financial assistance through Supplemental Security Income payments. It is worth the effort to investigate this possibility if this type of care is appropriate for your parent.

Getting the Big Picture

So, you can see that there are a wide variety and diversity of services available to help you and your family. But before you begin to seriously think about resource options, it is important to remember whose life is really under consideration here; although your parent's situation may be affecting your life, it is *their* life you are discussing and potentially changing. It is your mother who will go to the senior center, or your father who will go to adult day care. Therefore, it is imperative that they be involved in the process of sorting and choosing *their* options.

To go back to Peg, Ed, and Faith—what kinds of community services might be of help to them? Peg might talk to her mother about the possibility of getting her sister Martha to help finance a Meals-On-Wheels or homemaker service for her. Or perhaps she could go with her mother to the local senior center and see if the older woman might like to have dinner there a few times a week.

Ed's father might agree to have a social worker stop by and talk with him about what services might be helpful—and he might discover that there is a volunteer chore service in the community that would be perfect for the kinds of things he needs help with.

And Faith and her mother might visit the clergyman at her church and discuss the bereavement group that meets weekly. And while they are out, they might stop by the senior center and see what activities are going on—perhaps there is a monthly book club that the older woman would enjoy.

They all have many options—and so do you. *Resource Exercise III* will help you discover what some of your options might be.

Resource Exercise III

1) Get your needs lists from *Needs Exercises II* (their needs) and *Needs Exercise III* (your needs). As you review these lists you will see that all contain an empty column titled, "Resources." Now is the time to complete that column.

2) Get your resource lists from *Resource Exercise I* (your support networks) and *Resource Exercise II* (their support networks).

3) Review your resource lists and the section of this chapter on federal, state, and local resources, and fill in the resource column on all your needs lists.

a) Put down as many possible resources for meeting each need as is appropriate, regardless of whether you think a particular person would actually fulfill the need, or whether you think you could afford a particular community option.
b) In later exercises you will assess the actual possibility of each person or option meeting each need; the purpose of this exercise is to develop the outside parameters of all available resources.
c) Do not forget to consider whether the person who is the source of the need might be a possible resource for meeting—or reducing—that need.

* * * *

Again, the entire process of discovering resources is not one that can be done without your parents. You need to get them involved from the start. Perhaps this might involve talking to them about their feelings regarding their situation, and what they think can be done; you may be surprised to discover that they are aware of many resources you are not. Or perhaps this may mean discussing their feelings about growing old, or why they are reluctant to ask for help from a social worker. Perhaps you need to loop back to a number of earlier steps to help you decide on the best way to handle the situation.

So, where are you now? You are in a lot better shape than you were when you completed Step 3: Needs. At that point you were only aware of the overwhelming number of demands placed upon you, now you are also aware of the large number of resources available to help you meet those demands.

But there is a long distance between knowledge and action. Step 6 of The Balancing Act, Balance, and Step 7, Delegation And Action, will help you bridge that distance.

STEP 6
Balance

It's Not Easy Because It's Not Easy

How do you bridge the gap between knowledge and action, between your head and your heart? How do you find the fulcrum, the point of balance, from which you will derive the support to make the journey? You know you are overwhelmed by more needs and demands than any sane person has a right to assume. You know there is a wide array of people and agencies with resources available to help you. So, why can't you simply look down your needs column, and look down your resource column, and make the appropriate matches? Piece of cake—right? Easy enough—right? Wrong. To paraphrase Yogi Berra, "It's not easy because it's not easy."

There are a lot of reasons why it isn't easy. It's not easy to turn the tables and care for those who have cared for you—especially while caring for your children, your spouse, and yourself. It's not easy to face the reality of your parents' decline—or to face the reality of your own. It's not easy to accept the past and let go. It's not easy to accept the fact that you too have limitations. It's not easy to take a role with your parents that you hope your children will never have to take with you.

It's not easy for your parents either. It's not easy for a person who is used to caring and giving, to accept a new state of dependence. They may belittle themselves ("I'm worthless, poor me.") or belittle you ("Don't bother, your cooking's always too salty."). They may deny their physical decline ("I really can walk to the store in the snow.") or need constant reassurance that their neediness will not drive you away ("You won't hate me if I ask you to take me to Aunt Sally's again this Saturday, will you?"). They may glorify you ("You're a wonderful daughter—you can solve all my problems.") in a way that says it was they who made you the wonderful way you are, and therefore doing for them is really no problem for you. It's not easy to grow more and more dependent in a society that equates independence with worth—and dependence with worthlessness.

It's not easy from either side. And, overlying it all—for you and for them—is the fact that it's not easy to attempt to solve a problem for which there is often no happy solution.

But before you can begin to look for the optimum solution—to bridge the gap between knowledge and action—there are a number of realities that need to be faced and accepted. For some, facing these realities will be a trivial event, for others, one or more of these confrontations may be extremely painful. But it is highly unlikely you will be able to survive your Big Squeeze—to successfully move from knowledge to positive action—without looking these issues straight in the eye.

This step will help you accept some of the more difficult aspects of the reality confronting you:

1) Achieving filial maturity; accepting your parents for who they are, rather than who you wish them to be;
2) Recognizing your own limitations; accepting the reality of finite time and energy—and the realities of your relationships;

3) Setting limits without guilt; accepting that you *are* doing enough;
4) Supporting the efforts of others as they take responsibilty for their own lives: accepting that you cannot always be in control;
5) Acknowledging that there is no perfect solution: accepting that there are no correct answers to be discovered—only choices between better and worse options.

Filial Maturity

"I don't want to eat my dinners at the senior center," Mrs. Walsh said to her daughter Toni. "The food is barely edible, and Nora Doherty and Mary Hardiman are always talking, talking, talking."

"But you have to, Ma. There's really no other way. You can't stand well enough to cook for yourself anymore; and I can't cook for you either," Toni said gently. "And anyway, it's all arranged—I gave Mr. Syms a check for the next two months just this morning."

Mrs. Walsh looked at her hands and a tear rolled down her cheek. "I have no choice?" she asked in a small voice.

Toni knelt at her mother's feet and put her arms around the older woman. "Don't cry, Ma," she said, wiping away her mother's tears with the same gesture she had used on her son's tears earlier in the day. "Don't cry, Ma, I'll take care of you now. You don't have to worry about anything. It's my turn—I'll take care of you now."

* * * *

"I'm sorry to bother you, son," Bill Moffett's father said. "But I could really use a hand getting to Dr. Ehrlich's tomorrow. I could take the bus, but it's so difficult for me to walk to the bus stop with the snow and the ice, and it's not easy to climb the steps ..."

"What time's your appointment?" Bill just about growled into the phone.

"Two o'clock."

"I'll be at your house at one-thirty." Bill hung up and turned to his wife. "After the way he treated my mother when she needed him, he has a hell of a nerve coming to me now that the tables are turned! This is the last time—the last time I help the man who hurt us so much."

* * * *

Neither Toni nor Bill is responding to their parent in a positive way; Toni is reversing the parent-child roles and Bill is unable to forgive the past. Most likely, the end result of both actions will be frustration, anger, and resentment on the part of everyone involved.

Both Toni and Bill are victims of their own filial crisis: the ongoing recognition that a parent is no longer a source of support in times of trouble, but, instead, now needs the adult child for comfort and support. Toni and Bill have not accepted responsibility for their parent's needs in a positive way. They have not achieved filial maturity: the mature acceptance of the new interdependent relationship between parent and adult child. Their stories are examples of the two major pitfalls to attaining filial maturity: treating a parent like a child and staying caught up in old anger.

Filial maturity is the ability to accept your parents as they are—with their good points and their bad points. Filial maturity is the ability to recognize that your parents did the best they could do as parents, and as human beings—and accepting yourself in the same way. Filial maturity is not needing your parents' approval to know that you are okay.

It is not a role reversal

In many ways, the human aging process may appear to be a regression back to child-like dependency and fragility. Older people do often need help taking care of themselves, their mobility and memory may not be what it was, and, as is often true with small children, they may always seem to be sick. But the aging person is not a child; the aging person is an adult—an adult with a wealth of experience and a long history of self-sufficiency.

Your parents are not children, and your parents are not *your* children. To treat them as such is to devalue them—to strip them of self-esteem at a time when they are already losing so much.

Toni's mother's balance may be a bit off and her steps may be getting slower, but that doesn't mean she has regressed to the level of a toddler; she is the same adult she always was emotionally, mentally, and intellectually. She is still quite capable of deciding where, and with whom, she wishes to eat dinner—and she needs to be allowed to make that decision for herself.

If she could gain some perspective—and filial maturity—Toni might be able to see her mother as she really is: older and unable to cook for herself, but bright and alive and capable of making decisions. Then Toni would be able to see a quite different solution to the problem.

* * * *

"Ma, we have to talk about your dinners," Toni might say to her mother. "The truth of the matter is that—as much as we both hate to admit it—you can't stand well enough to cook for yourself, and I don't have the time to come over here every night."

Her mother might look at her sadly and nod.

"So what are we going to do?"

"I really don't like the senior center," Mrs. Walsh might say softly.

"I know you don't, Ma. But we may have no choice—unless you can think of another?"

"Meals-On-Wheels?" the older woman might suggest.

"I thought you didn't like the food?"

"Well, it is awfully bland ..."

"I know Ma," Toni might say. "I know that you're used to your own great cooking—and I know we've got two not-so-great choices here. But if we can't think of any other options, I guess you're going to have to choose between them."

The two women might sit in silence for awhile, and then Mrs. Walsh might sigh and say, "Maybe the Meals-On-Wheels won't be so bad ..."

"And maybe you can give me some of your recipes—I can come by on weekends and we can whip them up together," Toni might offer.

* * * *

Your mother's eyesight may be dimming, or she may spend more time alone in her apartment than you would like, or her arthritis may be slowly crippling her, but these things don't, in and of themselves, necessitate the loss of adulthood, the loss of self-sufficiency. When you treat your parents like children based on their physical abilities, inabilities, or disabilities, you take away the adult they have been, the major statuses they have always held and the major roles they have always played. They are already losing so much; they need to retain their dignity and self-esteem wherever and whenever possible.

The elderly need to be empowered, they need to know that although they are not able to walk as quickly or to see as well, they are still able to be functioning human beings; they are still able to make decisions about their own lives. When you can recognize that the grown-up, self-sufficient parent you have always known still resides inside a body that may be less able than it was, you will be well on your way to filial maturity. *Balance Exercise I* will help you start to assess how close to filial maturity you are.

Balance Exercise I

1) Think back to the last situation with your parent in which a decision about a specific action was required. Jot down the steps that were taken from the recognition that a problem existed, through the decision-making process, to the actual actions that were taken.

2) Ask yourself the following questions:

a) How was the issue isolated as a problem?
b) Who first recognized the problem and brought it to the attention of others?
c) Who was involved in the discussions?
d) Who was excluded from the discussions?
e) How was the final decision made (group consensus, individual, etc.)?
f) Who had the most influence on the final outcome?
g) Who put the decision into action?

3) Look at your answers to the questions above and ask yourself the following questions:

a) How many times does your parent's name appear?
b) How many times does your name appear?
c) Is this the way you would want your children to treat you?

Your answers to *Balance Exercise I* should start to give you some clues about the dynamics of your relationship with your parent. And it should also start to give you some clues about your degree of filial maturity.

Letting go of the past

Are you a perfect parent? Have you ever lost your temper with your daughter because you just had an argument with your husband? or your boss? or your own mother? Have you ever been too distracted by work, or a good book, or a TV show to listen—really listen—to what your son is saying? Have you ever hounded your children to study biology because you wanted to be a doctor, or to practice the piano because you couldn't afford to take lessons when you were their age? Have you always been there every time they needed you? Have you always said and done exactly the right thing to solve their problems? Well, your parents aren't perfect either.

There is no such thing as a perfect parent—although degrees of imperfection vary—and there is definitely no such thing as a perfect parent from the perspective of that parent's children. Your parents have made mistakes. You have made mistakes. You will all probably continue to make mistakes. Some mistakes are forgivable, perhaps others are not; the important point is that mistakes—yours and theirs—can be put behind you. You can all move on.

But you can't move on, you can't move beyond, you can't grow, until you can accept. Accept who they are. Accept who you are. Accept that some things cannot be changed. You can't change the past, but you *can* change how much you focus on it.

Filial maturity is about shifting your focus. Filial maturity is about accepting. Filial maturity is about letting go—of the frustration, the anger, and the hurt you feel because your parents were not (and perhaps still are not) the parents you wished them to be. And although some of your disappointment may remain, filial maturity is ultimately about recognizing and accepting that they were the best parents they could be—given who they are. Even if it wasn't good enough.

By the time you came into their lives, your parents were pretty much who they would be, they were already formed, their personalities, abilities, and outlooks had alreay been shaped by their childhood and adulthood experiences. They were parented too; they brought to their parenting a lot of the strengths and weaknesses their parents left to them—and their parents before them, and their parents before them.

Letting go is much easier when you are able to forgive. Perhaps your father worked too many hours, or your mother made you feel like you weren't as smart as your brother or as pretty as your sister—these are human failings, failings that occurred out of ignorance, and often with love.

It is much more difficult to let go of your anger when the things that they did were extremely harmful or hurtful. If your father abused you, or if your mother didn't love or approve of you, or if you grew up in a home affected by alcoholism—these things may be impossible to forgive. Even if what they did wasn't good—or even if it was bad—it was still the best they could do given who they were (they may have been abused, unloved, or brought up in an alcoholic family, too). It is not necessary to forgive what cannot be forgiven; it is only necessary to put it behind you, to let it go and gain some acceptance. Let go of the anger and, if necessary, let it be replaced by sadness and disappointment.

You can't change the past. You can't change the kind of parents your parents were—or the kind of parents they are. But you can change how you respond and relate to them. You can change and improve your relationship by letting go of the anger you feel about the things that cannot be changed; this will most probably make your expectations of them more reasonable—as well as your expectations for yourself (loop back to Step 2, if necessary). And maybe in the process you will be setting an example for your children—an example you may someday be very happy you set.

Mature adult acceptance

Filial maturity—mature adult acceptance of the realities of your family—is not easy to attain. It's hard for everyone, and it may be a long and extremely difficult task for many—too difficult for some.

If you find you are unable to do this alone—unable to let go of the anger, unable to release yourself from all the strong negative emotions you feel—it may make sense for you to seek outside help: a social worker, a gerontologist, or a therapist may offer the additional assistance you need. Remember, it is not necessary—it is not even advisable—to do any of this all by yourself. It *is* necessary—*and* advisable—to get the support that you need. It may be useful at this point to loop back to Step 5 to review all the resources you have.

Refraining from treating your parent like a child and letting go of the past are two giant steps toward filial maturity. These steps will lead you toward the creation of a more positive relationship built on interdependency—a relationship that fosters independence wherever possible, built on the honest recognition of each individual's present strengths and weaknesses.

Accepting Your Limitations

The super(wo)man myth

You can't do it all. Nobody can. You can't be the best mother, the best daughter, the best wife, the best worker, and the best friend. It is a physical and emotional impossibility. And perhaps, it is also a logistical impossibility, for often these roles are diametrically opposed. Often they contain within themselves contradictory expectations. Remember the good mother-daughter-wife dilemma discussed during the step on expectations? You may want to loop back and remind yourself of the paradoxes involved in this situation.

But what is the definition of the best daughter, best wife, best mother, best worker, or best friend? To some, the best daughter is the one who hovers over her father and makes his decisions and organizes his life; to others, the best daughter is the one who allows her mother the greatest autonomy and independence. What you define as *best* may not be the best.

In some ways we are all children still striving to please Mom and Dad—that's how we learned to become social beings, and that's how we acquired our ideas of what is *best*. This isn't bad—it's normal. But it can have negative effects if you don't understand where your ideas of *best* came from—and if you don't have the insight to see whether these ideas are appropriate to your present situation. You may want to loop back to Step 1, Awareness, and think about this.

Perfection is found in fairy tales, not in real life. Superman and Superwoman are in comic books, not at the office or the supermarket or the nursing home. Energy and time are finite; you need to accept that you cannot do it all. *Balance Exercise II* will refresh your memory about your own often unrealistic expectations for yourself.

Balance Exercise II

1) Get all the needs lists you developed from *Needs Exercises II and III*; you are going to repeat the last three steps of *Needs Exercise III*.

2) Take all the lists and sit down in the middle of the floor. Start with your own list and place it in front of you. As you did before, place the other lists in a semi-circle in front of you. Remember: you now are surrounded by all the needs that are squeezing you.

3) Look at all the pages, at all the items, at all the hours, how does this make you feel?

4) Add up all the hours you have estimated would be necessary to meet everyone's needs in an average week, and answer the following questions: Could any single person possibly accomplish this? Do you think a person should expect

to be able to meet all of these needs? If you have answered *no* to *a* or *b*, ask yourself why you think you can do it—never mind should you.

* * * *

But, once again, intellectually recognizing that you are placing too many demands on yourself is very different from taking action toward reducing those demands. One of the first steps between recognition and action is understanding where you got the idea that you could do it all in the first place.

> "My son can do anything," Mrs. Warnock bragged to her friend Sayde. "My daughter-in-law works all the time; he takes the kids to school, does the food shopping, the yard work, cooks—and he calls me every morning just to say hello."

> "You are a truly amazing woman," Gil Sturgis said to his wife, an admiring smile on his face. "I don't know how you do it, but you do. Sometimes I think you could do just about anything!"

> "Did you see the article about that woman in the paper yesterday?" Lynn Civetti asked her friend, Louise. "She's a physician, has three kids, and just finished her second novel—if she can do that, I can take care of my two kids and my mother; after all, I only work part-time."

* * * *

Super(wo)man messages come from everywhere: John Warnock got the message from his mother, Elaine Sturgis got the message from her husband, Lynn Civetti got the message from the media. You probably get the message from these sources and many others—including yourself. Often, other's messages are reflections of what you expect of yourself.

You hear the message, it sounds good, you believe it: you can do it all. The problem is—the messages are wrong: no one can do it all. And there is absolutely no way anyone can do it all well. Loop back to the awareness and expectation steps—they may give you some additional clues as to where your super(wo)man ideas came from.

The 'good enough' child

Sometimes being a *good enough* child is better than being the *best* child. For example, *good enough* might be better than *best* when your definition of *best* is impossible, or when your definition of *best* is not what is *best* for your parent, or when your definition of *best* child interferes with your ability to perform your other roles.

* * * *

"My mother is coming up tomorrow to stay with us for two weeks," Lois Flavin told her friend Abby. "I'm making a pact with myself that this time will be different; I won't lose my temper, and we won't have any arguments. Everything will be perfect—we're going to be a happy-go-lucky family. It is going to be a wonderful visit—even if it kills me."

* * * *

"I'm sorry, honey" Judith Cannon told her daughter. "I've got to stay at Grandma's and keep her company while she eats dinner so I won't be home until late. Do you think you could whip up some spaghetti, or hot dogs, or something for you, and Dad, and the boys? I promise I won't be later than eight o'clock—I'll help you with your homework then."

* * * *

Lois Flavin is setting herself up to fail. She and her mother have had an adversarial relationship since she was a toddler; they have never spent two days together without arguing—let alone two weeks. She would be better off planning a *good enough* scenario (where a more positive, yet possible, situation is envisioned), rather than a *best* scenario (where everything is based on an unachievable perfection). For example, perhaps she could make a deal with herself that she would not raise her voice when she and her mother argued, or that she would not slam out of the house, or that she would not say hurtful things. Any of these *good enough* solutions are possible and within her control. Ultimately, the *good enough* solution might enhance her mother's visit; Lois' *best* solution most likely will not.

And maybe Judith Cannon's *best* daughter actions (which necessitated staying at her mother's while the older woman ate) could be improved by a *good enough* approach that allowed her to get home in time for dinner with her own family.

Do these scenarios sound familiar? Are you ever guilty of trying to be too good? It may not be easy to accept, but often, being *good enough* is the best you can be—for you and for them.

Limit Setting Without Guilt

You know there is too much to do and too little time to do it. You know you can't do it all and that it is probably best for all involved if you don't. But, how do you do it? How do you pull back in a way that you can feel okay about? How do you do it in a way that doesn't leave someone hanging over the abyss with no support? How can you be a *good enough* child without feeling like a bad one?

Finding the fulcrum

Providing too much support takes away power, providing too little support can have equally disastrous effects; the trick is finding the fulcrum, the point of balance where everyone gives and receives in the needed amounts. Obviously, this is a very difficult task; not only is it hard to figure out the right amount of support, but that right amount is constantly in flux.

So are you setting yourself up for another failure? Is this another unachievable goal? Not necessarily—not if you are willing to give up some control, not if you are willing to negotiate and share responsibility, and not if you are willing to allow your family to be run democratically rather than dictatorially.

The goal is for no one—not your child, not your parent, and not yourself—to be a dictator. It's perfectly fine to expect, to even demand, that everyone be flexible and willing to accommodate themselves to the needs of the others—even a 5-year-old can be expected to lower his voice if Grandma is sleeping, or to pick up his toys so Grandpa won't trip; even your mother can be expected to understand that your teenage daughter needs her privacy. The goal is not individual autonomy, but an interdependent set of relationships based on mutual respect and tolerance.

The next chapter will discuss getting your family together, and developing more democratic methods of handling family problems. The remainder of this chapter will focus on your individual relationship with individual family members.

Respecting their choices

You are who you are. Your mother is who she is. Your son is who he is. Each person needs to have control over as many aspects of his or her life as is possible—and every other person needs to respect this control and the choices that come from it. A family can't be *managed*; each person must be allowed to participate in the decision-making process—especially the aging parent.

* * * *

> Stan Brokmeier got a call from his mother early one morning. Elma, the live-in aide he had hired to care for her, was tying her to her bed at night; she felt imprisoned, like a criminal, in her own home. Stan took a sick day and drove the three hours to his mother's house.
>
> When he got there he found both his mother and the aide waiting for him. Elma told him that his mother was walking

in the night, and could easily fall down the stairs and break a hip. Elma reminded Stan that he had only hired her to work from 7:00 a.m. to 7:00 p.m.; there was no choice, in order for Elma to sleep, Stan's mother had to be restrained in her bed.

Mrs. Brokmeier said she didn't care if she broke her hip; if she did—so be it. Nothing was worse than being treated like a prisoner. It was her life and she had the right to decide how she wanted to live it.

Stan told Elma not to restrain his mother, spent the day visiting, and drove home after dinner. He knew he was taking a risk; but it was the risk his mother had chosen.

Two months later, with Elma asleep in the next room, Stan's mother fell during one of her nocturnal wanderings. She broke her hip and required surgery; she did not survive the anesthesia.

Even in his grief, Stan knew he had done the right thing; his mother had lived her last months the way she had chosen, rather than living her last years in a prison he had chosen for her.

* * * *

Stan made the more difficult of the two choices. It would have been easier for him to decide that his mother needed to be physically safe; he could have justified his decision as the *right* thing to do, and he could have felt less guilt. But he didn't. He took the more difficult road: the road that showed he really understood his mother's needs and desires; the road that showed he respected her as an individual with the ability and the right to make decisions about things that affected her life and well-being.

Finding the fulcrum works the same way with your children, your spouse, your job, your friends; by releasing control, and empowering others, you can start to see where you can pull back. If your 8-year-old daughter thinks she can walk home from school alone, perhaps she can. If your husband thinks he can buy his own ties, perhaps he can. If your father thinks he can cook his own meals, perhaps he can. They are empowered, and suddenly you have three less things to do tomorrow afternoon.

So what if your daughter steps in all the puddles? So what if your husband's eye for style and value is not the same as your own? So what if your father makes himself a pan of chicken four nights in a row? None of these choices require you to take over. It is their choice and they—not you—are responsible for the consequences. You don't have to protect them—or yourself—from the results of their choices. It is your husband's tie, your daughter's feet, your father's dinner.

* * * *

Darlene Graf was furious with her parents. She was certain the best thing for them was to move into a beautiful retirement community just minutes from her home. She had spent weeks investigating every possible residential option, and now that she had found the perfect solution they were refusing to leave their small apartment in a run-down area of the city. Stubborn old mules, she thought to herself.

Then, to make matters even worse, Darlene's 18-year-old daughter suddenly announced she wasn't going to the college she and Darlene had so carefully chosen; instead she was moving across the country to work as a waitress with her friend Martha. Darlene was beside herself: why was it she worked so hard for everyone and no one appreciated it? Why was it that she was always fighting with the people she was trying to make happy?

* * * *

Darlene's problem is that she is trying to be responsible for everyone and not letting her parents or her daughter be responsible for themselves. Darlene is setting up control battles she cannot win. Darlene's parents are responsible for themselves. Darlene's daughter is responsible for herself. It is not Darlene's responsibility to make their decisions for them. Her desire to help may stem from her love for her family, but Darlene is tearing her family apart by not recognizing and respecting their individuality or their right to make their own choices. Darlene needs to step back and find the fulcrum—and you may need to do the same.

Setting limits

In some cases you need to set limits on yourself; you are doing too much. In other cases you need to set limits on them; they are demanding too much, or interfering too much, or expecting too much (loop back to Expectations and Needs). Neither situation is easy and both require communication.

As was true for many other aspects of your Big Squeeze, the key to all limit setting is communication (loop back to Communication). You have the right to set limits—on your parents, your children, your spouse, and yourself—but no one will respect these limits if you don't communicate them.

* * * *

Justine Antiqua was in the middle of her morning shower when her daughter Krissy came into the bathroom and started a long tirade about her mother's decision not to let her sleep over at her friend Nan's that evening. When Krissy sulked off for breakfast, Justine's husband replaced her on the bath mat; he wanted to discuss the details of his upcoming business trip. After he finally left the room, Justine sighed in relief. She climbed out of the shower and began drying her hair.

Next, her mother—who lived with them—walked into the bathroom without knocking and started gossiping about her friend Mabel's daughter's son's girlfriend who had been arrested for drunk driving the previous evening.

Justine threw the hair dryer down on the sink with a loud whack and turned to her mother. "Please give me a few moments of peace," she said through clenched teeth. "Can't I have a moment of privacy—even in the bathroom?"

Flustered and hurt, Justine's mother left the room.

* * * *

Justine has every right to expect privacy in the bathroom; but, as she had never expressed this desire to her family, no one thought of it as an intrusion. She thinks everyone knows about her feelings—but they obviously don't. The result of her lack of communication was unnecessary anger and hurt. Often, in trying to be there for everyone, in trying to meet everyone's needs in a limited portion of time, you set yourself up. Maybe this was an old family habit, or maybe Justine never realized it bothered her before, or maybe she never had the courage to mention it to anyone.

Whatever the reason, Justine needs to be clear with her daughter, her husband, and her mother that the bathroom is off-limits; if she presents her request in a direct, non-threatening manner they will respect it, and she will have some peace. If she doesn't tell them, there will be many more mornings of anger and frustration.

Setting Limits on Them. Your 6-year-old son interrupts every time you talk to someone on the phone. Your wife expects you to do her mother's yard work, take out the older woman's trash every week, and be generally available to run her errands. Your father expects you to call him every morning to make sure he doesn't need a ride to the doctor or the pharmacy. Are these behaviors unreasonable? Possibly. Are they annoying? Decidedly. Is there something you can do about them? Definitely.

Your son might be looking for more of your time and attention. Your wife is—although perhaps unconsciously—taking advantage of your good nature. And your over-dependent father—also perhaps unconsciously—is using guilt to get your attention. Although you may be well aware of the justifications for their behavior, it is perfectly acceptable to say no to unreasonable requests. And sometimes it may be perfectly acceptable to say no to reasonable requests.

Unfortunately, saying no is not easy. But, if the rejection is offered along with some creative problem-solving, together you might be able to come up with some alternatives that meet everyone's needs. Perhaps your son can be quieted with the promise of a little *alone time* after each telephone call he does not interrupt. Perhaps together, you, your wife, and your mother-in-law might find that the older woman is capable of doing some of the things herself, and that if she keeps a running list—rather than expecting you to show up at the drop of a hat—you might be willing to come by on Saturday afternoons and tackle the chores one-by-one.

Setting Limits on Yourself. The reasons adult children get caught up in over-doing for their parents are often complex. Again, these reasons can vary from fear of loss and death, to repaying the parental debt, to needing to be needed (loop back to Awareness). But above and beyond these issues, there is another cause for over-doing: a desire for the parents' final years to be happy, often coupled with a desire for their approval.

If you are an adult child who is comfortable with your parent, and content with the kind of parenting you received as a child, this desire for your parent's happiness may be direct and sincere. But you also have to be aware that it is *not* your responsibility to make your parent happy, and, in many cases, it is impossible for you to do so.

If your mother is sad and lonely following the death of your father, but never was a particularly outgoing or social person, coercing her into going to the church bingo games is not going to make her less lonely; fixing her sadness may be out of your control. If your father has painful arthritis, there is not much you can do to make his joints hurt less; it is out of your control. If the kids in school are teasing your son because he's very short, there is not much you can do to change his physical stature; again it is out of your control. It is important to recognize that you can't always fix it.

This is not to say that you can't help, that you can't increase their happiness or comfort, it is only to say that you might be setting yourself up to fail. Therefore, you need to set limits on what you can reasonably expect from the situation, limits on what you can reasonably expect from yourself—based on what they, and you, really need (if necessary, loop back to Step 3).

These limits then need to be translated into actions, but not any actions, they need to be translated into actions that you can live with—without guilt. And the key to reducing guilt is not promising too much—to yourself or to them. Much guilt comes from unfulfilled promises—try not to make any you can't keep.

Things are even more difficult for the adult child who has a less-than-perfect relationship with his or her parent. Even those who have attained filial maturity, and let go of the painful parts of the past, are often motivated by a complex set of conscious and unconscious emotions.

The son who never felt love or approval during his childhood may strive for that missed approval at this late point in his mother's life. Consciously or unconsciously, he may think that by doing and doing and over-doing for her, maybe now, maybe finally, she will come to recognize and appreciate her wonderful son. Unfortunately, the mother who didn't appreciate her child for 50 years, will probably not appreciate that child now.

Again, this is not to say that you shouldn't try to make your parent's life easier or happier if you can, but you might be setting yourself up to fail, once again. If this sounds at all familiar, think about why you are doing what you are doing, and ask yourself if it makes sense.

Is your disapproving father going to turn approving if you call him everyday, or will he just find something else to disapprove of? Will your unloving mother suddenly turn all warm and affectionate if you shop for her, and cook for her, and clean her house? If the answer is no, rethink why you are over-doing (perhaps loop back to Awareness and Expectations), and begin to set some more reasonable limits for yourself—limits you can put into action without guilt.

Perhaps the most difficult situation is to be the child of a parent whose behavior is so reprehensible that you are caught in a tug of war between feeling you owe him nothing and feeling there is still an obligation that you must meet. If your parent was willfully abusive, or neglectful, or if his behavior was truly unforgivable, you do have the right to set limits on your involvement with him.

If your parents now demand more of you than you think they rightfully deserve, you may wish to set limits on your behavior based on your history. Maybe the extent of your responsibility is to call a social service agency, or to give your parent some money, or to set up a few needed services.

You do have an obligation to your parent, but that obligation may be limited; it may be concrete, rather than emotionally-laden; it may not be as large as your parent would like. You may find that there are things you can do—and things you cannot do. For example, you may find you are able to handle the tasks your unloving and critical mother *needs* done, but that you unable to handle an evening of pseudo-friendly conversation. If you can accept both her limitations in the past and your own in the present, you will be able to gain some comfort with your level of response.

It is up to you to assess your situation and, based on the past and present realities of that situation, to honestly decide what you can expect from yourself. Then you need to translate that reasonable expectation into a reasonable action—an action you can take without guilt.

Interpreting Limit Setting. There is one final aspect of limit setting that can be very difficult to handle: what do you do when your parent sets a limit on you that you don't want to live with. Do you have to abide by limits set by others?

* * * *

Karen Raskin put down the phone and burst into tears. For the second time that week her father had refused to come over for supper. Karen knew that her father resented her renewed commitment to her career—and her new job. He felt that her place was at home with her family—which included his having dinner with them at least three times a week. Their tradition of frequent and leisurely, multi-course family dinners had changed into hasty meals of pizza or Chinese take-out—accompanied by the older man's frowning face.

Before hanging up, her father had told Karen he was going to start having dinner at the senior center—where the food was less salty and the atmosphere more relaxed—so she needn't bother to invite him for supper anymore.

* * * *

Did this mean she can't ever invite him for dinner again? Does Karen have to do what her father says? Does one person have the right to set limits without regard to the feelings of others? The answer is no. Limits need to be negotiated among all the players, and sometimes, where they haven't been negotiated, a contrary response may be necessary to begin the process.

Both Karen and her father are responsible for themselves, they are each responsible for doing what they want to do. If Karen wants to invite him, she should do just it—or perhaps one of the grandchildren should call. They may find he is more than happy to join them for dinner—once his anger has cooled down a bit. You might find the same in a similar situation.

There's No Happy Ending

Probably the cruelest truth that you must face is that your Big Squeeze is a story without a happy ending. The reality of the situation is that the tale ends when your parents die; it ends with you as an orphan.

That is the truth; it's not pleasant, it's not happy, but it *is* the truth. You are in the midst of a dilemma for which you will be unable to find a solution; there is no correct answer, no ideal action, that will change the inevitable end. You are faced with choices, none of them perfect—perhaps none that even feel good—but they are the choices from which you must pick.

Accept the reality of your situation and you give yourself a fighting chance of finding the fulcrum, of achieving the balance you need to survive. Deny it and strive for perfection and you will spend a lifetime striving—and you will still fail.

STEP 7
Delegation And Action

It Can't Be Done Alone

Lindsay Doerr received a call from her mother late one night; her grandmother was very ill and had been hospitalized, the doctors didn't know what was wrong, but the older woman was running a very high temperature and they had placed her on the critical list. After notifying her boss and arranging for the children to be picked up from their various activities for the next few days, Lindsay flew down to be with her grandmother.

Her mother and aunt were sitting immobile and terrified in the room with their mother when Lindsay arrived. Lindsay quickly assessed the situation and immediately went into action: she called in the nurses, made appointments with two of her grandmother's doctors, began dictating orders to her mother and aunt, and rushed to her grandmother's apartment to cook up a big batch of chicken soup.

When Lindsay returned to the hospital with the soup, her grandmother ate it (the first thing she had eaten in two days), began to let the nurses help her to the bathroom, and generally perked up. Lindsay patted herself on the back for her efforts; her mother and aunt were profuse with their thanks. But when the two daughters took it upon themselves to decide where their mother should go after she left the hospital, Lindsay nixed the decision as silly and inappropriate—and cancelled their orders.

After three days, Lindsay had to go home. She promised she would return the next weekend (and every weekend after that), and would oversee her grandmother's care by long-distance telephone. She didn't see the glares of animosity that her mother and aunt shot at her retreating back when she finally left the hospital.

* * * *

Beatrice Selinsky was running herself ragged, but she had no choice. The only child of a widowed father who was in the early stages of Alzheimer's, the parent of two teenage boys and a college-bound daughter, and the wife of a salesman who was constantly on the road, Beatrice's life was a whirlwind of activity and demand.

She rose before dawn to get her father dressed and fed before she dropped him at adult day care on her way to work, spent nine hours in the office—more often than not interrupted by some kind of minor family crisis, then came home to housework and chores that lasted until midnight. She didn't know how she was going to keep going; she only knew that she had to.

Beatrice chose to ignore the cold that she developed. She continued to ignore the symptoms even when she felt dizzy and light-headed. She resisted all suggestions that she see a doctor, claiming she had no time to be sick. One afternoon, Beatrice just about collapsed at work; her friend Jean brought her home and took her temperature: 103 degrees. Beatrice ended up in bed for a week with a very bad case of the flu.

* * * *

Lindsay's over-doing caused anger and resentment on the part of her mother and aunt, and will most likely lead to overload for her, which will most likely lead to anger and resentment on the part of her husband and children. Beatrice's over-doing landed her in bed, leaving her father, her husband, and her children with no support at all.

Caring for an aging parent—or grandparent, or uncle or aunt—cannot be done alone. It's not good for you (overload), it's not good for your parent (strips them of power), and it's not good for the rest of your family (they don't get to contribute). But one of the saddest effects is that often the stress of the overload deprives both parties of the pleasure that can result from the positive aspects of spending more time together.

* * * *

Jake Cantrell couldn't believe it: he and his father had actually spent an afternoon together and had had fun; it reminded him of the camping trips they had taken together when he was a boy. His father's eyesight had been failing over the last year, and Jake had been spending more and more time helping him with his household and physical needs. But it seemed that the more time they spent together the worse their relationship got.

Jake knew it was partially his own fault; he knew he was not in the best mood when he rushed in on his way home from work to help his father with dinner, or bathing, or picking-up the apartment. But who could fault him? He had a growing business, and a growing family, and he was only trying to do what needed to be done to the best of his ability.

It had actually been a big blow-up with his wife that had straightened out the whole thing. She had demanded that they all sit down together and figure out a way that he could spend more time at home with her and the kids. They called Jake's sister and father, and between the four of them they came up with a plan combining a Meals-On-Wheels service with a bi-weekly cleaning service and a round-robin of transportation and visiting from the three adult children.

Jake's father was happier because he didn't have to listen to Jake grumble (and he thought the "girl" who delivered the Meals-On-Wheels was really cute), Jake's sister was happier and less guilty because she was helping, Jake's wife was happier now that Jake was home more, and Jake was happier because he was much less pressured. But best of all, now that Jake was freed up from the more tedious aspects of caring for him, he had more *quality time* to spend with his father, and as a result, they were rediscovering the great relationship they had enjoyed when he was a boy.

* * * *

The truth is that, in most instances, the aging parent does not just belong to you; he or she belongs to the family. And the family—all family members, not just you—may be more available to help, and may want to help more than you think. But you will never know until you let them get involved.

It's a Family Affair

The same way a child is best nurtured surrounded by a close-knit loving family with a mother, a father, grandparents, aunts, uncles, and cousins, so too is an elderly person best nurtured when surrounded by a family that cares. This isn't to say that a child brought up without an extended family, or by a single parent, cannot become a happy successful adult, but the life chances for success and happiness are better within a positive family environment. This is also true of the elderly.

There are some instances where this is impossible, perhaps due to a small number of living relatives or irreconcilable differences between family members. If this is true of your situation, many of the specifics that follow will not directly apply to you. But even if there are *no* other family members to be considered, the basic steps outlined are the same.

1) Clearly identify the problem.
2) Discuss the problem with your parent.
3) Bring in anyone else that might be of assistance. (If there is little or no family, doctors, social workers, gerontologists or representatives of community agancies might be included.)

4) Get everyone together to set priorities and assess resources and commitments—as a group, with your parent's desires and inputs as primary.
5) Make the necessary decisions—again, as a group, with your parent's desires and inputs as primary.

It's Best for Your Parent. Your aging parents are the primary recipients of the benefits of making their concerns and issues a family affair. Again, it is important to remember that your parents are in the midst of a very important, and often very difficult, stage of their life cycle. They are most likely undergoing a series of losses—their bodies are giving out on them, their statuses are disappearing, their friends and loved ones are dying—while they are trying to come to grips with the reality of their own rapidly-advancing mortality.

Your parents needs an anchor, a sense of belonging, a place where they know they will receive positive support. They need their family, a family that stretches as wide and as deep and as far as possible, a family that is braided together in a way that provides a support network that is stronger than any of its single strands could ever be.

It is difficult to grow old, to try and adjust and adapt to your own changing abilities amidst a world filled with changing demands, expectations, and resources. Your parents are struggling to integrate their past with their present and with their sometimes not-so-rosy future; they are trying to make that final transition with bodies and minds that, in many cases, are not what they used to be.

They need help, and the job is too big for one person; they need the help and support of everyone who cares about them. When more family members are involved there are more messages sent: "we love you," "we care about you," "you are important to us." The positive effects from this type of wide-spread love and support can not be underestimated.

You are all helping them make some difficult decisions—or at least helping them acknowledge that a difficult situation exits. It will be much easier for them to face these sometimes harsh truths if their whole family is there to support them.

Your parent is also a member of the family; by making it a family affair this fact is reinforced and your parent becomes a participant in the decision-making and task-allocation processes. When aging parents are actively involved, they are less resistant to the final decision (because they participated), display increased self-esteem (because they were consulted and respected), take on more responsibility for helping themselves (because shared decision-making often leads to increased involvement), are more content (because of all of the above), and often even live longer, healthier lives.

It's Best for You. It goes without saying that sharing the responsibility for both decision-making and caretaking is going to have many positive effects for you. Research has shown over and over again that the negative impacts of caring for an aging parent without adequate support can be pervasive and severe: mental illness, physical illness, marital problems, job problems, difficulties with children—all of these can go hand-in-hand with an over-stressed, under-supported caregiver.

When you let go of control, delegate, and allow others to get involved, you decrease your load and reduce the chances that any of the negative effects just mentioned will materialize. An added bonus is the probability that you will enhance your relationships with your family.

Making the Best of a Tough Situation Is Best for Everyone. The advantages of making it a family affair extend to everyone involved. Quite often, those who have not been engrossed in the situation feel guilty, and sometimes even frustrated with you for not *allowing* them—right or wrong—to contribute their ideas, time, or skills.

It is important to remember that a support role is more than just carrying out delegated tasks—it is also having a part in deciding what needs to be done. Give your parents, your siblings, your spouse—even the grandchildren—a chance to voice their opinions, their needs, and their expectations.

You may need to reach out to those who are not doing—whether because of distance or lack of interest. You need to talk to them, to let them know that their ideas and help are needed. Include them; you may be surprised to find they are more receptive than you thought they might be. This can have the effect of both cutting down on their feelings of guilt and frustration, and transforming them from observers into participants by way of their active involvement in the decision-making process.

And, by involving more people in the decision-making and support process, you will most likely cut down on your chances of making mistakes. When a number of people are involved, things are discussed before the fact, and the situation is viewed from multiple perspectives; this often leads to better solutions. In addition, when the whole family is involved—including the aging parent—there is a lot less chance of actions being thought of as "meddling," and a lot more chance of the actions being accepted in a positive way, by all those concerned.

Sharing the decision-making process also distributes and disperses some of the burdens involved in coming to grips with these often difficult choices. If the decision was painful (placing Mom in a nursing home or taking away Dad's driver's licence), the pain and guilt can also be shared. It wasn't just your decision, it was a family decision; perhaps not a happy solution, but a solution derived from thought and consideration, and arrived at through mutual consensus. Sharing also helps if a mistake had been made (Mom didn't get the care she needed at the nursing home, or Dad fired the housekeeper you all pitched in to hire); again, it was not your mistake alone—the burden, the blame, and the guilt are all shared, and thereby made easier to bear. You all did the best you could; it wasn't perfect, but it was your collective best.

Getting the extended family system to work

The goal of this step is to maximize interdependence among all the members of your family. Note the use of the word *maximize*—meaning optimize, striving to encourage your extended family system to work *to the best of its ability.*

The goal is not a perfectly-functioning extended family—remember, perfection is an unachievable goal—the goal is to get everyone to contribute at the maximum level possible, given the reality and constraints of who and what your family is, and the problems under consideration. As with many of the goals outlined in this book, this too is not easy to attain, but there are a number of things that can be done to increase your chances of success.

The first step toward successful family interdependence is everyone's recognition that this is a family affair, that this is not a situation that belongs only to one daughter or even to all the adult children, that this is a situation that belongs to everyone—from the oldest adult to the youngest grandchild. And most importantly, this is a situation that centers around your parents. Therefore, everything you do as a family needs to be focused on your parents: their perceptions, their views, their ideas, their preferences. If they are not able to articulate these things, do what you all feel would be what they would prefer.

Family interdependence cannot be achieved without communication—and face-to-face communication is clearly the best kind (variations for families where this is not possible will be discussed later). Therefore, in order to start dealing as a family unit, you need to get together. And, in order for this get-together to happen, someone needs to take a temporary—not permanent—leadership role. Someone needs to raise a red flag and declare that you all have a problem that needs to be discussed as a family.

Usually this role falls to the person who first recognized that there was an overload situation—perhaps your parent, or perhaps yourself. Often it is the person who first called, "Time out, I need some help here." In most cases, this person must be willing to do some of the initial groundwork to get the family together. He or she must also be willing to relinquish or share the leadership once the group is assembled.

Another obvious prerequisite for getting the family together is that a reasonable number of family members be willing to participate in, as well as abide by, group decisions. For some families this may be two (you and your parent), for others it may involve twenty (parents, and siblings, and spouses, and grandchildren). For some families this may be no problem, for others it may be very difficult.

But even if you have a temporary leader, and an adequate number of people who agree that decision-making is positive and possible, your chances of success will be further enhanced if a certain number of family traits are present. This is not to say that if your family doesn't have these qualities you are doomed, but these are the characteristics you should try to encourage.

Adaptability among family members is a key to successful decision-making. Although it would be unusual to find a family in which all members had this characteristic, flexibility can be learned and encouraged through role-modeling, group pressure and, sometimes, just the act of being involved in a group which places a strong value on compromise.

A realistic and sensitive viewpoint among family members regarding the needs and situation of the aging parent is also a plus. And your chances of success will be further increased if family members are sensitive enough to be able to tell the difference between the times when intervention is necessary and those when it might be more useful to just let things be. In addition, if your family exhibits a mutual commitment to honesty, compromise, and open communication, the job will be much easier.

But what if your family doesn't conform to this ideal? (And most probably don't.) In some cases, perhaps the situation cannot, and should not, be made a family affair. For example: if there are no relatives; if your family is so conflicted that a get-together would produce such chaos that the probability of a positive outcome is extremely remote; if, for some reason, a family get-together would have negative emotional or physical effects on the parent the get-together is supposed to help; or, if a family get-together would have negative emotional or physical effects on you.

If any of these situations are true in your case, than you should probably consider alternatives. Perhaps you should just have an honest and open conversation with your parent about the situation. Or maybe a get-together comprised of yourself, your parent, a doctor or a social worker, would be the most useful approach.

In all other cases—even if your brother Joe refuses to come, or your sister Alice has never compromised with anyone in her life, or Melanie and Malcolm are still angry about what happened in Ann Arbor last year—it is still preferable to attempt a family get-together. And don't postpone it until a serious crisis throws everyone—including you—into a panic. The chances are, since you are reading this book, there are enough problems and issues to warrant a family get-together right now.

The Family Get-Together

As every family is unique, with its unique members and problems, so too is every family get-together going to be unique—from how it is planned, to the form that it takes, to how decisions get made, to how actions are taken. Some get-togethers may be an informal discussion over a couple of pizzas; some may be quite formal, involve a number of professionals, and take place in a gerontologist's office. Some may include only a single adult child and a single parent; some may be large extended-family affairs. Some may be difficult and combative; others may draw the family closer together. Some may involve all of the activities that follow; others may include only one or two.

As with The Balancing Act itself, there is no wrong or right way to have a family get-together; there is no absolute order that the events must follow. It, too, is a process that involves looping, and jumping, and finding the steps and methods that work best for your unique situation—and your unique family. So, just read what follows with an eye for picking and choosing the pieces that make the most sense for you.

For example, in some cases, it might make sense to do the first few activities by yourself—before you bring the whole family together. If all your siblings live out of town, and you have been the only one involved in your comatose father's care—it may make the most sense for you to get all the information from his doctors before the family drives 200 miles to your house for a get-together.

In all cases where it is possible, it is best for your parent to be involved right from the start; but the way that your parent responds is going to affect how the get-together unfolds. For example, if your mother thinks it's a great idea, you will easily be able to work out a plan together; but, if she feels it is completely unnecessary—and is angry and insulted that you would even suggest it—a different set of actions will need to take place. This may involve some looping to previous steps: Is it their need or your need? Is it your expectation or theirs? Is a get-together even necessary? How can you get them to recognize that it's important for them to do it for you?

In some cases it might make the most sense for your two brothers to organize the get-together because you just don't have the time. In others, perhaps the get-together should be called first for everyone to decide collectively what the first actions should be.

Other aspects of the get-together (where to have it, when to have it, who to include, etc.) will also be dependent on your particular situation. If your widowed mother has been suddenly paralyzed by an unexpected stroke, your options will be quite different than if your mentally-alert, but slightly-arthritic father needs help figuring out the best residential community for him.

The rest of this chapter details some general guidelines for setting up and carrying out a family get-together. Again, although these guidelines are organized in a step-like sequence, it is not necessary for you to follow them in the exact order listed. For example, if you, your three sisters, and their husbands have all come together to decide what to do about Mom's failing eyesight, planning the logistics and deciding who to include in the get-together, is obviously unnecessary. Or, if your father is being released from the hospital at the end of the week, but is obviously unable to live unattended, you are all too aware that the immediate problem is figuring out where Dad should go next Friday, and defining the problem, is superfluous.

It is important to remember that the family get-together is not a solution in-and-of itself; the family get-together is not an end—it is a means to an end. It is a means toward group problem-solving and family interdependence. Hopefully, it is a means toward helping your family discover a better way to deal with your problems, a means toward helping your family develop a flexibility that will allow you all to adapt and respond—in a positive, collective way—as your situation changes.

It is also important to be aware that, while you have learned a lot about expectations, awareness, and communication, the others have not. And because of this, their emotions may get played out during your family get-together;

expect this and let it happen. But if it gets too hard to handle, don't be afraid to stop. Don't be afraid to ask for professional assistance if you think that is what your family needs. There is a lot of help out there—and the key to surviving your Big Squeeze is taking advantage of that help whenever, and wherever, you can.

Avoiding mistakes up front

There are a number of mistakes that families make when confronted with the increased dependency needs of an elderly parent. Although many of these have been discussed previously, and some will be discussed in more detail later, they bear noting here; for if these issues are addressed and understood before the get-together begins, you will considerably enhance your chances of success.

Common Mistakes Regarding Your Parent. The most common, and perhaps the most deadly, mistake that families make is overestimating the needs of the older person while simultaneously underestimating the elder's ability to take care of himself. This mistake often results in a vicious cycle of unnecessary sacrifice and *over-functioning* on the part of the adult children, and an increased withdrawal, passivity and *under-functioning* as a self-fulfilling response by the parent; this parental response often increases and perpetuates dependence and decline.

There are two things that will decrease the chance of your family falling into this trap: Whenever and wherever possible, include your parent in every aspect of the process—they have a moral and a legal right to participate in discussions and decisions that affect them—and always frame your thoughts, questions, and decisions in terms of what Mom is able to do, rather than what Mom is unable to do.

Another mistake commonly made is for families to assume that the symptoms of confusion, anxiety, hostility, or depression that their parent is displaying are the necessary result of the aging process. This is often *not* the case. These symptoms may be normal responses to a difficult, strange, or unpleasant situation. Put yourself in their place: if your spouse recently died, and your children wanted you to leave the home you have lived in for 40 years, wouldn't you be depressed?

These symptoms also might be side effects of medication. Or they might be caused by the very family problems that are bringing you together. Put yourself in their place again: if your son was angry with you for needing him to take you to the doctor three times a week, and your daughter was angry with your son because he was taking too much control, and your son-in-law was angry with both of them, wouldn't you be anxious and a bit hostile?

Making promises to your parent that you can't keep can also have devastating effects that can undermine any success you might otherwise achieve. Don't promise your mother she will never have to go to a nursing home (you may think this is true, but you can never be sure); do promise her you will visit her wherever she is living. The emotional promise *to care about* ("Don't worry Dad, I will always care about Mom.") is very different from a promise *to take care of* ("I promise you, Dad, I will always take care of Mom."); and the former is much easier to keep. Three clues to avoiding the unkeepable-promise trap are: avoid the use of the words *ever*, *never*, and *always*; think before you make any promise; and never make a death-bed promise unless you are *absolutely positive* it is one you can keep.

Common Mistakes Related to the Get-together. Again, in order to increase the chances of the success of the get-together, everyone needs to be supportive of an open, honest, and flexible exchange of ideas; if this concept has not been agreed to from the beginning, you are setting yourselves up for failure. A common mistake is not to state this goal up-front, and failing to set up the necessary ground rules for it to happen.

If possible, the family should agree that no relevant secrets will be kept, no relevant feelings hidden (except where they might be detrimental to the goals of the group), and all will strive to let go of old animosities for the purpose of positive, collective problem-solving. If it is impossible to get everyone to agree to these guidelines, get agreement from as many people as you can.

A mistake that families often make—or the person who organizes the get-together often makes—is to assume that the get-together will result in an equal distribution of responsibility. Because of individual differences in resources and commitment, this is usually an impossibility. Don't assume equity; assume some form of participation by all. And, wherever possible, accept whatever is offered.

Families are often resistant to change—old patterns of power and collective action are deeply ingrained. You are faced with a new and unique problem for which these old styles may be inappropriate. For example, the brother who had always assumed leadership because of his business success, may be at a complete loss when dealing with emotional problems, and the sister who was never taken seriously because she didn't go to college, may be the best equipped to lead the family through this sensitive crisis. A family that was dominated by a dictatorial patriarch, may now have to shift to a more egalitarian, shared leadership style. Flexibility and openness to necessary changes are the keys.

Another common mistake, linked to resistance to change, is sticking to the rigid stereotypes you have developed of each other over the years. Nora is "the good one," Nancy is "the smart one," and Naomi is "the selfish one." Family members often receive one-dimensional labels which, aside from being unfair, tend to increase animosity and decrease the family's ability to maximize the use of all the resources of its members. Forget past labels and look at the whole person; let each be the person she really is.

Another mistake many families make is rushing into permanent solutions at a time when a more flexible, temporary solution might make the most sense. Chances are you are not dealing with a static situation, but with a situation that is in a constant state of flux. And to make matters even more complicated, it is often quite difficult to anticipate many of the upcoming events.

Will your mother recover the use of her left side, remain partially paralyzed, or suffer another—perhaps even more debilitating—stroke? The best solution is to deal with the immediate problem, while developing a flexible long-term plan that can branch and adapt itself to new situations.

Common Mindset Mistakes. Don't expect miracles. Do expect resistance. Do expect it to be difficult, but do expect some successes. Don't expect a perfect solution. Do expect to work hard. Do expect to feel anxious. Do keep your sense of humor. And do keep reminding yourself that this is the only family you've got.

Getting the information you need

Again, you might be managing this activity by yourself, with your parent, with one or two others, or this may be the task around which the family get-together is organized. Whatever the specifics of the situation, the process is essentially the same: collecting and refining the information necessary to define your problem. The primary sources of this information are your parent(s), professionals, and family caregivers.

Obviously, the entire family will need to be included when it comes to specifically labeling the problem; at this stage of the game, the information is being collected as a way of helping you lay out what the parameters of the problem are. Is your mother going to be able to live on her own? Is your father ever going to be able to walk? Are there enough supports in the community so your father can stay in his apartment, or do you need to find out if he can afford the near-by retirement community? What are your mother's preferences? What's your sister's schedule? What's your range of options?

If information has already been collected from your mother's doctor on her condition and prognosis, from a social worker on community resources and sources of financial assistance, from your parents on their perceptions and desires, and from the family caregivers on their levels of demand and availability, the get-together will move forward more quickly and efficiently.

Again, the most crucial source of information is your parent. It is your mother's life you are making decisions about; she needs to be at the center of the process. If, due to physical or mental constraints, she is unable to participate, you must do the best you can to figure out what she would prefer; letters, living wills, and discussions with her friends and close family members are good sources of this kind of information.

If, due to physical or mental constraints, she is unable to be at the actual get-together, her input is even more important to obtain at this point in the process. Find out what your mother thinks, feels, and desires, then give her what she wants—or as close to it as you can possibly get.

Your parent has probably come into contact with a number of professionals who will have insight into his or her needs, abilities, and prognosis. Consult as many of these professionals as possible, for these multiple perspectives (which may or may not present a similar picture) will give you the widest possible view of the true situation. Books, friends, and social service agencies may also be a source for information on financial assistance, living options, or community support. Other elders—or your friends who have elderly parents—may have information that will be of help to you.

Unfortunately, in many cases, the information you get will be neither clear nor conclusive. The experts may disagree.

There may be no way of knowing exactly how your mother's cancer will turn out. Your father's financial situation is in limbo. Your sister doesn't know whether she will have a job next year or not. The same way there are no easy, straight-forward answers, there are often no easy, straight-forward questions. Expect this, and do the best you can. Your best *is* good enough.

Planning

Obviously, you cannot have a family get-together without deciding who will be included, or when and where it will be held. Again, this may be a decision you are making yourself, with your parent, or with a few family members. Again, this is a family affair, and everyone's interests and constraints should be taken into consideration.

Who to Include. In some families the question of whom to include at the get-together will be relatively trivial, in others this issue may cause significant problems. A basic rule-of-thumb is to be consistent: include all siblings and their spouses, or include just the siblings, or include everyone—including children old enough to participate effectively.

You may also want to include other close family members, friends, or professionals who you can assume are either very concerned with your parent's well-being, strongly affected by or involved with your parent's situation, or have specific resources that may be of assistance—in conjunction with a willingness to use those resources.

Review the genogram you made during *Awareness Exercise I* and the resource lists you developed during *Resources Exercises I and II* to make sure you have included everyone you want involved.

When and Where. If at all possible, hold the get-together at your parent's home; this centers control where it should be—with your parent. If this is not possible, the second choice would be the place to which your parent has the easiest access. Other alternatives might be the most centrally located home or a professional's office.

When to hold the get-together becomes a matter of finding the most suitable time for all. If it is impossible to find a time that accommodates everyone, set up a time that is convenient for the majority and get input from those who can not physically be there.

The get-together need not be face-to-face. Although this is the best option, if financial, time, or geographic considerations make a face-to-face get-together an impossibility, a conference call might have to suffice. This solution may not be optimum, but it is workable.

Starting off on the right foot

Now that everyone is together, there are a number of things that should be done at the beginning to increase your chances of success.

If it is at all possible, one or both of your parents should take the leadership role; this is their life under discussion, and they deserve to control the get-together—as well as all other aspects of the situation—as much as possible. If they are present, but for some reason are unable or unwilling to take this role, give them the seats at the *head of the table* and defer to them at every step.

If a person other than your parent does take leadership, it is important that he or she state—right from the beginning—that they are in this position temporarily, and that democratic decision-making and shared leadership is the goal.

It is important that the get-together begin with some kind of statement of purpose; this statement need not be formal, just clear. For example, are you gathered together to decide where your mother will go after she is released from the hospital on Sunday? Or to decide whether she is still capable of living on her own? Or to decide what her future living options are? Or to develop a schedule for multiple get-togethers that will hopefully result in a plan for her long-term living situation? Each of these different goals will result in a different type of get-together. A common understanding of why you are all gathered needs to be developed.

There are also a number of ground rules and assumptions that are helpful to make clear from the beginning.

1) Everyone will be given a chance to speak and express their opinion and personal situation;
2) Everyone will be listened to and—conversely—allowed to respond;
3) The object of the get-together is to help your parent find the best possible solution to the problem—even if it is not the solution any other family member wants it to be;
4) The solution will be reached in a democratic fashion, and compromise is likely to be necessary—unanimity may be the goal, but a majority decision, strongly weighted toward the wishes of your parent, will suffice;
5) It is unlikely that there will be a perfect match between the parental needs and the family's available resources;
6) A difficult, perhaps turbulent, discussion with an imperfect solution may be inevitable;
7) And finally, this may be the first in a series of get-togethers, but all of this is okay.

It may also be helpful to discuss how you see the events of the get-together unfolding. Most family get-togethers will start with the most stressed-out member saying, "I asked everyone here because I feel overwhelmed by how things are going." But beyond this, the way each family goes about dealing with the problem will most likely be different. A possible scenario might go something like this:

1) Your parents present their perception of the situation;
2) There is a discussion of all the information collected from doctors, social workers, etc.;
3) Each family member presents his own perception of the situation;
4) There is an open discussion of the problem;
5) The family resources and commitment are determined;
6) A plan is developed.

Figuring out the problem

In some situations the definition of the problem may be relatively straight-forward: your father, who refuses to cook for himself, keeps firing the housekeeper, and a decision needs to be made about how he will get his meals. In some situations defining the problem may be very complex—Is it really Alzheimer's or just the medication? If it is Alzheimer's what does this mean for the future? What are the support options? Your problem may be very specific: where is the best place for Mom and Dad to live? Or it may be quite nebulous: Is Mom really able to manage alone, but pretending that she can't; or is she really unable to manage alone, but pretending that she can?

And, to make matters even more complex, it is not just the immediate problem that needs to be defined—often there are long-term problems or decisions that need to be planned for.

It is during this part of the get-together that all the information needs to be presented—in a straight-forward, non-judgmental manner. Your parent should speak first, followed by the person reporting the information collected from professionals and other sources, followed by the caregivers discussing their perceptions, followed by all the other family members—including proxy statements. Each person should be given the respect of being listened to, and no impressions or ideas should be automatically discarded this early in the process.

Then each member of the group should be allowed to give his or her impressions and opinions as to: what they see the exact nature of the problem to be; what they think the short and long-term aspects of the situation are; what they think the priorities should be; and what they think the focus of this particular get-together should be.

It is important that everyone listen, and that everyone gets an opportunity to express their thoughts and feelings.

Reaching an agreement as to the exact nature and scope of the problem may prove to be more difficult than you expect. You may think the problem is your mother's failing eyesight. Your father may think the problem is the bad ophthalmologist your mother has been going to. Your mother may think the problem is the dials on the appliances in her kitchen. And your sister Margaret may think the problem is your desire to control everybody's life.

It may be necessary for someone to take a leadership role—optimally your parent—to try to clarify the situation as much as possible. This may involve:

- the tactful elimination of unrealistic proposals—there is no point discussing the problem of keeping your mother's apartment clean when it is apparent that she can no longer live alone;
- a restatement of family member's comments;
- a breakdown of the problem into its component parts—component one: where should Mom go next week; component two: where should Mom go for the next six months while she is unable to walk; component three: where should Mom go after she is able to walk but still may be unable to live by herself.

Once the problem has been defined and broken down into its component parts, it is necessary to decide which pieces need to be handled at the current get-together, and which pieces should be set aside for a later date.

After this, an additional step may be necessary to prioritize the pieces of the problem you have decided should be discussed at this get-together. For example, if you know ahead of time that resources are limited, what is more important, arranging transportation for your mother to get to church or to the senior center? Obviously, in this situation the decision should be your mother's.

Discovering resources and commitments

You have now all agreed on the scope of the problem, which pieces of the problem you are going to deal with during the get-together, and how to prioritize the smaller points of the problem—you have defined one side of the equation. Now is the time for you and your family to define the other side: what are the available resources to meet the problem—and who is willing to commit to what.

Beginning with your parent, let each person answer the following questions:

1) What are their capabilities and resources?
2) What are their existing commitments?
3) How much do they feel it is legitimately possible for them to offer to do?
4) What are they realistically able and willing to do?

Again, each person should be encouraged to be as honest as possible, and each should be allowed to speak without interruption. When everyone is finished you will have a rough idea of what everyone is willing to contribute. Now it is time to make some decisions.

Making decisions

As a family, you have defined the problem. You have broken it down into its component parts. You have prioritized the issues. You know where the resources are. You know what each member is willing to commit. Now you must put it all together: another difficult, but do-able, task.

At this point, a restatement of some of the important underlying assumptions may be useful. Remember, the goal is a flexible plan that looks to the future, that branches and allows for alternatives and change, but that is currently focused on the immediate situation. The primary consideration is your parent's desires; in all possible instances, decisions and actions should fall to your parents. Although unanimity is desired, it is not required—compromise and sacrifice should be expected. And once a decision is made, even if it is not unanimous, everyone will abide by it.

It may also be useful at this point to restate the problem, and list the alternatives and options you have discussed. Once again, starting with your parent, let everyone speak, voicing his or her ideas, opinions, and suggestions.

Be prepared for this to be a long part of the process; disagreements and arguments may erupt, power struggles may develop, some people may actually get up and leave. Everyone should help to keep the discussion open, honest, and as free of conflict as possible.

In the best of all possible situations, the end result of this process will be a group decision that, even if not unanimous, and even if not *perfect*, is an acceptable, realistic solution supported by, and binding on, all involved.

But what if you don't have the *best of all possible situations?* What if you have worked through the equation and there is no way the problem matches the available resources? What if your mother has stormed off in a huff? What if your brothers' simmering rivalry boiled over into a fist fight? The only solution is to pull back, regroup, and try again.

But next time, try it with a new twist: meet in a different setting, get more information, let everyone cool down and think things through. Perhaps your approach was too unclear, and a more definitive statement of the issues and problems would be productive. Or maybe your approach was too cool and business-like, and a more informal tossing around of ideas would be appropriate.

Sometimes an outsider can serve as a mediator; a doctor, social worker, gerontologist, or clergy member might be able to arbitrate a dispute, or shed a different light on the situation, thereby allowing the family to come together and try again. Maybe some one-on-one diplomacy might bring your errant brother back to the fold, where group pressure just pushed him out. Or perhaps family therapy would be of assistance.

Another alternative is a strong dose of positive family time. *Delegation Exercise I* might be of some use in bringing your family closer together.

Delegation Exercise I

1) Invite all your family members to a family dinner, preferably at your parents, but anywhere without negative or power connotations will do. Include all children and spouses, and set a light, happy tone for the meal.

2) Ask everyone to bring photograph albums, scrap books, old movies, videos, momentos—anything that evokes positive family images for them. You may be touched to learn that your parents saved your second-grade report card, or that your sister still has a letter you sent her from Vietnam.

3) Share with each other all the things you each have brought. Show the children old pictures and tell them family stories and reminiscences.

4) Draw a genogram together, and explain to the children how you are all related to each other.

5) Enjoy.

* * * *

Hopefully, one of these solutions will work for you, and you will be able to hold another family get-together with a more positive outcome.

Action and adaptation

The problem has been defined, a solution has been outlined, tasks and responsibilities have been allocated. Action—and acceptance and adjustment to the agreed-to actions—is now necessary on everyone's part. Your mother must accept that John can't come running every time she has a leaky faucet. You must accept that you can't control what your father eats. And your sister Jenny must accept that it is her responsibility to have Mom come stay with her every other weekend—even if she would rather go to the beach. You must all do it, and you must all accept the new realities with good grace. Granted, this is difficult, but it is also possible.

An even more difficult, and less controllable, aspect of the situation is its state of flux; you and your family are precariously balancing on a bed of molten lava, you are not standing tall on an immobile ledge of rock. There is so much that can change: your mother can get sicker or your father can get healthier, your brother-in-law may get transferred to a distant state or you may become embroiled in a divorce. The downside of interdependence is that anything that affects one of the interdependent members, by definition, affects the others, and the precarious equilibrium of the system. The upside is that there is a lot of support.

Your mother gets sicker; you have to revise the plan because she can't leave the nursing home on the weekends. Your father gets healthier; you have to regroup and devise a housing situation for him now that he is going to survive. Your brother-in-law gets transferred and your sister Joan, your mother's first-string caretaker, is gone; you need to reorganize the support systems between yourself and your brother.

You become embroiled in a divorce; your siblings readjust and pick up more of the load while you are too emotionally drained to be of much help.

Your Big Squeeze is a situation of continual change, one that requires adaptation and the flexibility to do what is necessary—and then move on. Now you have set up a way to allow this to happen—together, as a family.

* * * *

> Mildred and Stan Collyer had been arguing for the past year over the way Stan's parents—according to Mildred —"manipulated" him. Despite Stan and Mildred's pleas for the older Collyers to move out of the city, Stan's parents remained in a dingy apartment in the run-down neighborhood where Stan had been born.
>
> The urban streets were dangerous, and the elderly Collyers were afraid to go out after dark; the roof leaked in the bedroom; there were mice in the kitchen; and the landlord was never to be found. So they called Stan.
>
> They called Stan at least twice a week. First thing in the morning: could Stan please stop by and shovel the icy steps? Last thing at night: Dad was having chest pains, could Stan come down and help? And Stan always went—even though it took him over an hour to drive back and forth. They hardly ever called Stan's sister Roberta; she lived closer to them, but it was dangerous for a woman to drive into the city alone.
>
> Finally Stan and Roberta convinced their parents to move out to the suburbs; the four of them spent many weekends searching the want-ads and tramping through apartments. Now Stan was home even less; he was still running into town to help his parents with their day-to-day problems, while spending his weekends trying to find them a new place to live.
>
> But Mildred didn't mind, assuming the end would justify the means. The problem was that every apartment had some unacceptable flaw; nothing seemed to satisfy the older Collyers. It soon began to dawn on Mildred that nothing ever would.

Mildred's proverbial final straw occurred late one morning when Stan's mother called him in a panic: she had had her purse snatched—she was so upset and overwrought that someone had to come immediately. Unfortunately, neither Mildred nor Stan could get away from work and Roberta's son was running a temperature of 103; Stan was forced to arrange for his daughter Lara to leave school and drive down to her grandparents'. Mildred called a family get-together.

Mildred, Stan, Roberta, Roberta's husband Michael, and three of the five grandchildren met with the elder Collyers at their apartment. Mildred began the meeting by stating that she was finding it all to be just too much. That although she loved both Mom and Dad dearly, the way they were choosing to live their lives was causing her—and her family life—to suffer.

It wasn't easy and it wasn't fun, but together they explored the older couple's needs, the family's combined resources, and everyone's pre-existing commitments.

Stan's parents finally admitted that they were unwilling to move from their apartment. Stan admitted that he could not be at their beck and call when they lived so far away. Roberta admitted she felt guilty about Stan carrying all the responsibility. Mildred admitted her anger and frustration with the entire situation.

Collectively, they explored alternative options: homemakers, handyman services, and elderly transportation. The elder Collyers said they didn't want strangers around. Stan reiterated that they lived too far away for him to come running every time they called; as long as they choose to live in the city he would be unable to be their first line of support, but he would be able to help them set up alternative services. He told them that they could always call him, but that he would not always be able to come.

Roberta said she could come by on Saturday afternoons, Lara said she could be available every other Sunday, and Stan and Mildred helped them set up a support network including a list of telephone alternatives for when Stan was unavailable: 911, Dr. Haverson, Boston Cab, and Hub Elder Services.

No one was thrilled with the solution, but—over time—they all came to accept it. After the early kinks were worked out, there were a number of surprising and happy results. The elder Collyers found that—once they got used to it—they enjoyed their new independence. Stan felt a little guilty about the whole thing, but he felt good about supporting his parents in the decision they choose—and he also knew he would want his children to do the same for him. Roberta and Lara felt good about doing their share, and Mildred and Stan stopped arguing.

And Roberta just called everyone to invite them over for dinner next Sunday and talk about a long-term plan so that they will be better prepared for any issues that may arise in the future.

* * * *

Things stabilized for the Collyer family and, although they knew there would be future crises, they also knew that they now had the means to deal with them. The family get-together worked for Stan Collyer and his family. It can work for yours too.

STEP 8
Maintenance

Congratulations. You are now well on your way to surviving your Big Squeeze. You know who all your players are, and where you all stand in the life cycle. You are alert to the emotional issues the situation ignites within you. You can distinguish between overt and covert expectations. You know how to tell the difference between stated and actual needs. You have a better understanding of the communication patterns that you and your family use, and how to improve upon them. You are familiar with the many personal and community resources available. You can accept the reality of finite time and energy, and the need for delegation and letting go of control. You have held a family get-together and developed an interdependent plan for handling the situation. Your family has allocated tasks and put them into action. Now all you have to do is hold on to it all.

As with so many issues discussed in this book, holding on—maintaining the fragile stability—is not an easy task. In some ways, your situation is analogous to that of the person who has just ended a long diet: you have successfully achieved an extremely difficult and energy-consuming goal—one which can only be maintained through constant vigilance and a change in your approach to how you live your day-to-day life.

As the dieter has to completely revise his or her eating habits and remain always aware of the new changes, so you too must revise and remain aware. It's easy to slip back into old emotions and patterns. To once again take control and begin to do everything yourself. To reverse roles and treat your parent like your child. To stop listening for the covert message. To forget what and who else might be out there to help you.

It's hard to stay on top of it all, to be aware, accepting and cognizant of your own tendency to err. It's hard; but it has to be done if you want to survive your Big Squeeze. Remember, your Big Squeeze isn't a one-shot deal; most likely, your Big Squeeze is for a long, long time.

The Pitfalls

"Oh, Dad, this is a disaster," Ellen Nilsen said, grabbing a sponge and attacking her father's kitchen counter. "I'll do it—I'll just do it myself. I can't stand seeing you living in this squalor."

Her father shook his head sadly. "Looks fine to me."

"That's because you can't see," Ellen snapped as she dropped to her knees and began sweeping crumbs from the floor into her hand.

* * * *

Although she had agreed to give it a try, Amanda Kinnear fired every housekeeper her sons hired. The first one was nasty. The second one didn't clean the toilet. And the third one stole her pot holders. The fourth one didn't even wait for Amanda—she saw it coming and quit on her own.

Amanda used the martyr silent-treatment on her sons when they came to discuss the issue with her. She didn't perk up again until her daughters-in-law returned to their previous system of coming by to clean on alternating Thursdays.

* * * *

Not wanting Gramps to go into a nursing home, Scott Dunham and his cousin Zachary promised to spend Sunday afternoons keeping the older man company and giving him a hand with whatever he needed. At the family get-together, Susan and Sandy—Scott and Zachary's mothers and Gramp's daughters—had been skeptical about this commitment. But the boys, who were very attached to their grandfather, swore up and down they were absolutely positive it was a commitment they could keep. Until hockey practice. Until ski season. Until wrestling. Until Adam Horner's party.

Before they realized it, Susan and Sandy were thrust back into the caretaker role that had previously overwhelmed them—the role that had caused them to call the family get-together in the first place. But they knew the boys were just kids who needed to have fun—and anyway, they told each other, Gramps was *their* father.

* * * *

All three of these families had come so far, just to slip back into the old, unworkable patterns. Ellen couldn't keep herself from taking control and treating her father like a child. Amanda's sons and daughters-in-law allowed Amanda to manipulate them back into a situation that was easier for her—although more difficult for them. And Susan and Sandy let the caretaker role fall onto their shoulders once again, erroneously assuming it to be a daughter's task—not a family affair.

What could they have done to stop the slide? What can they do to correct the situation? They can integrate the emotional and practical lessons of The Balancing Act into their way of life. They can learn to internalize the ongoing process of The Balancing Act and use it whenever necessary.

How can they—and you—accomplish this? Through vigilance, awareness, and looping.

Looping

Flipping back to Page 17, you will see that The Balancing Act is a circle of eight interconnected steps. There is no final step—although this step is labeled as number 8—rather, the process keeps looping and returning back to each and every one of the previous steps.

These feedback loops are the essence of The Balancing Act, and the core of this step: the ongoing, as-needed replay of earlier lessons to help you achieve flexible and responsible—if temporary—solutions.

And remember, The Balancing Act focuses on both the emotional *and* practical aspects of your situation. You will most likely have trouble organizing a family get-together if you let your fear of your parents' death, or your need to be needed, interfere with your ability to honestly communicate with your mother. Your Big Squeeze is not just a problem of logistics; it is much more than just that. It is a problem rooted in complex individual and family emotions; if you forget this fact you are destined to lose the lessons of The Balancing Act.

For, as your Big Squeeze continues and changes, you must adjust both your emotions and your behavior. No single family get-together, no single awareness, no single decision is going to provide the answer for long. A dynamic, changing situation demands an adaptable, flexible method to meet it. And it also demands adaptable, flexible people to enact it.

Each family's situation will be different, and therefore demand a different pattern of looping. Perhaps Ellen Nilsen should loop back to Step 6 and reconsider her level of filial maturity. Amanda Kinnear's sons might benefit from a loop back to Step 2 to analyze their mother's covert and overt expectations, and then perhaps loop down to Step 4 to better understand how Amanda is communicating her real feelings to them. It's pretty obvious that Susan and Sandy need to loop back to Step 7 and hold another family get-together, a get-together focused on everyone's realistic ability—rather than desire—to meet their commitments. And they all need to think about the emotions the situation raises in them at every step.

And, as the situation is not static, neither is the looping. Ellen may loop back to Step 6 and refrain from cleaning her father's kitchen, but find that two months later he isn't eating. Now she has a different problem—and different emotional reactions—so she must loop back to Step 1 to reassess her awareness and to Step 3 to reassess what his current needs actually are.

As for Amanda's sons, after looping back to steps 2 and 6, they may discover that they are confronted with an untenable situation, and need to loop to Step 7 and hold another family get-together; the focus of this get-together might be Amanda's choice between accepting a housekeeper or giving up her apartment.

And these solutions will create new situations, which, when coupled with outside changes, will create new problems, new emotions, and new dilemmas. Problems, emotions, and dilemmas that, when addressed by looping through the appropriate steps of The Balancing Act, can be confronted and resolved—for the moment. Until new situations and new feelings arise and continue to arise, and arise, and arise. And new patterns of looping are enacted to meet these new situations again, and again, and again.

It is this on-going process that will enable you to survive your Big Squeeze. Surviving means finding the best possible mesh between each person's need for independence and their simultaneous necessity for interdependence. Surviving means finding your fulcrum, your balance, so you are stable and flexible enough to be able to be there for your parents, your children, your spouse, and yourself. Surviving means holding on to your sanity—and your personal life—and letting everyone else hold on to theirs.

Appendices

Evaluating a Continuing-Care Facility

After determining that a continuing-care facility is an option for your parent, develop a list of reputable facilities in your area. Good sources for this information are your doctor, social service agency, social worker, church or synagogue, parent, friends, and parent's friends relations. Ask them all for the names of places they would recommend. If it is at all possible, involve your parent in this process--he or she is the one who will be living there, and his or her desires are primary.

After building your list, contact the nursing homes or continuing-care facilities by telephone. Ask for a social worker, and give him or her the following information:

1) Describe your parent's condition—including any physical or mental limitation.
2) Give a recent history of your parent's condition, particularly noting the rate of change or the degree of stability.
3) Discuss the anticipated sequence and timing of relevant events.

Now it's your turn. Ask the following questions:

1) Do you have adequate programs and staff to care for my parent?
2) Is this a single-or multi-level facility?
3) Do you accept Title XIX (Medicaid)?
4) Are you Medicare Part B certified?
5) What is the process of admission?
6) What is your ratio of staff to patients?
7) When can I come and look over the facility?
8) Will you be the person to show me around?
9) If you are unavailable, who do I see?

If the information you have gathered is satisfactory—i.e., the social worker answered all your questions honestly, and the answers met your specific needs—make an appointment to inspect the facility. It is best to visit at least four or five places, so you have an adequate basis of comparison.

Be on time, and bring your spouse or a friend; four eyes and ears are better than two. Bring this questionnaire with you, and be prepared to take notes. Don't be afraid to ask hard questions and press for more information where you feel it is necessary.

1) Is there a license on display?
2) Does the administrator have a current state license?
3) Is the Patient's Bill of Rights posted?
4) What is the ratio of RN's and LPN's to patients on each shift?
5) What is the ratio of aides to patients on each shift?
6) Are the employees unionized?
7) How many beds are there, and what is the current population?
8) What personal possessions can patients bring, and are they protected?
9) Where and how often can patients shower, and are they alone or with an attendant?
10) What areas of the facility and grounds are available to ambulatory patients?
11) What areas of the facility and grounds are available to non-ambulatory patients?
12) Are there ramps or elevators?
13) Do you have a continuing program for patients who are confused and disoriented?
14) Do you have an active recreation program, and how many staff people oversee an activity?
15) Do you have a site facility and staff for physical therapy? occupational therapy? beautician services?
16) Where do patients receive medical treatment? podiatry? optical service? dental service?
17) Do consultants visit? How often?

18) Do patients have access to a pharmacy? What are the hours?
19) Do patients have direct access to a laundry? a convenience store? television? telephone?
20) What is the daily routine, and is a written schedule available?
21) Can private physicians be retained?
22) Is there ready access to outside outings? shopping? meals?
23) Is storage or preparation of food permitted?
24) What are the visiting hours?
25) Are there special parties on birthdays and holidays?
26) Is leaving the premises with a responsible person permitted?
27) Is there presently a waiting list? How many names are on it? Approximately how many months does that represent?
28) Are there private rooms available? If not, is there any choice of roommate? What is the cost difference?
29) Is there a reference list of family members of past and present residents available?
30) What are the strengths of this facility? What are the weaknesses?
31) Is there anything special or important to keep in mind about this facility?

Once you have gathered all the information possible, put it all together and read it carefully. Discuss it with your parent, spouse, doctor, and anyone else who might have special insight into the problem. Don't make a hasty decision, and don't underestimate how emotionally difficult this situation is.

Interviewing a Homemaker

When selecting a homemaker, be thorough, and ask for the following preliminary information:

Name:

Address:

Phone number:

1) Why are you interested in this job?
2) What experience do you have to qualify you for this job?
3) What training do you have that is pertinent to this position? Home Health Aide Certification? Red Cross CPR Training?
4) What do you like about working with older adults?
5) What problems have you run into working with older adults? How have you handled them?
6) Under what circumstances would you feel it necessary to call a doctor? 911? me?
7) What do you do with older adults who need help eating? bathing? dressing? How do you handle these situations?
8) Are you willing to do general housekeeping? laundry? marketing? meal preparation and clean-up?
9) Do you drive? Do you have your own car? Are you comfortable driving the person you will be caring for? Do you have a history of motor vehicle violations or accidents? Is your car insured?
10) Ask for a resume and three references (at least two should be work-related, not personal).

Following this preliminary round, ask these addition questions.

1) Are you presently employeed? How long have you been there, and why are you leaving? (If the applicant is not currently employeed, ask these questions about their last position.)
2) Describe your duties on your current or last job.
3) What did you like about your last job? What did you dislike?
4) Would your last employer say you are hardworking? dependable? punctual?
5) Is there anything in particular you have found difficult to do, or that you prefer not to do?

If the applicant gets this far, consider these general points:

1) If possible, have the person to be cared for meet the applicant. Note their interaction, and heavily weigh the elders input.
2) Does the applicant seem compassionate and kind?
3) Does the applicant seem to possess the qualities you deem necessary for this job (i.e., physical strength, ability to cajole, good sense of humor, high-frustration tolerance, etc.)?
4) How does the applicant communicate? Is this adequate for the job?
5) How do you feel about the applicant?
6) Call *all* the references and listen carefully to what they say.
7) Take your time, and interview as many people as possible.

Bibliography

Adelmann, Nora, E. *Directory of Life Care Communities.* New York: H.W. Wilson, 1981.

Ball, Avis Jane. *Caring For An Aging Parent: Have I Done All I Can?* Buffalo, NY: Prometheus Books, 1986.

Baulch, Evelyn M. *Extended Health Care at Home: A Complete and Practical Guide.* Berkeley, CA: Celestial Arts, 1988.

Becker, Howard. "Personal Change in Adult Life." *Middle Age and Aging,* Neugarten (ed). Chicago: University of Chicago Press, 1968.

Bettelheim, Bruno. *Dialogues With Mothers.* New York: Avon, 1962.

Bloomfield, Harold, and Leonard, Felder. *Making Peace With Your Parents.* Boston: Shambhala Publishing, 1987.

Brenton, Myron. *How to Survive Your Child's Rebellious Teens.* New York: Lippincott, 1979.

Breytspraak, Linda M. *The Development of Self in Later Life.* Boston: Little, Brown, 1984.

Brody, Elaine, and Norah Dempsey and Rachel Pruchno. "Mental Health of Sons and Daughters of the Institutionalized Aged." *The Gerontologist,* Vol. 30, No. 2, 1990.

Brown, Robert N. *The Rights of Older Persons: An American Civil Liberties Union Handbook.* New York: Avon, 1979.

Bumagin, Virginia, and Kathryn F. Hirn. *Aging is a Family Affair.* New York: Crowell, 1979.

Caplan, Paula J. *Don't Blame Mother: Mending the Mother-Daughter Relationship.* New York: Harper & Row, 1989.

Chapman, Elwood. *The Unfinished Business of Living: Helping Aging Parents Help Themselves.* Los Altos, CA: Crisp Publications, 1988.

Cicirelli, Victor G. "A Measure of Filial Anxiety Regarding Anticipated Care of Elderly Parents." *The Gerontologist,* Vol 28, No. 4, 1988.

Constantine, Larry L. *Family Paradigms: The Practice of Theory in Family Therapy.* New York: Guilford Press, 1986.

Cox, Harold (ed). *Aging,* 4th Ed. Guilford, CT: Duskin Publishing, 1985.

Directory of Alzheimer's Disease Treatment Facilities and Home Health Programs. Phoenix, AZ: Oryx Press, 1989.

Directory of Childcare Centers, Vol. 1. Phoenix, AZ: Oryx Press, 1986.

Directory of Nursing Homes, 3rd Ed. Phoenix, AZ: Oryx Press, 1988.

Dychtwald, Ken, and Joe Flower. *Age Wave.* Los Angeles, CA: Tarcher, 1989.

Edinberg, Mark A. *Talking With Your Aging Parents.* Boston: Shambhala Publishing, 1987.

Edye, Donna R., and Jay A. Rich. *Psychological Distress in Aging.* Rockville, MD: Aspen Systems Corporation, 1983.

Erikson, Erik (ed). *Adulthood.* New York: Norton, 1976.

Erikson, Erik. *Childhood and Society.* New York: Norton, 1950.

Fox, Nancy. *You, Your Parent and the Nursing Home: The Family Guide to Long-Term Care.* New York: Prometheus Books, 1986.

Friedman, Jo-anne. *A Complete Guide: Home Health Care;* New York: Norton, 1986.

George, Linda. "Models of Transitions in Middle and Later Life." *Annals, AAPSS,* No. 464, 1982.

Ginott, Haim G. *Between Parent and Teenager.* New York: McMillan, 1969.

Gold, Margaret. *Guide to Housing Alternatives for Older Citizens.* New York: Consumer Reports Books; 1985.

Goldstein, Marion Zucker (ed). *Family Involvement in Treatment of the Frail Elderly.* Washington, DC: American Psychiatric Press, 1989.

Greenberg, Vivian. *Your Best is Good Enough.* Lexington, MA: Lexington Books, 1989.

Halpern, James. *Helping Your Aging Parents: A Practical Guide for Adult Children.* New York: McGraw-Hill, 1987.

Hamon, Raeann R., and Rosemary Blieszner. "Filial Responsibility Expectations Among Adult Child-Older Parent Pairs." *Journal of Gerontology, Psychological Sciences,* Vol. 45, No. 3, 1990.

Herr, John J., and John H. Weakland. *Counseling Elders and Their Families.* New York: Springer, 1979.

Herriott, Martha, and Asuman H. Kiyak. "Bereavement in Old Age: Implications for Therapy and Research." *Journal of Gerontological Social Work,* Vol 3(3), 1981.

Hill, Reuber. "Decision Making and the Family Life Cycle." *Middle Age and Aging,* Neugarten (ed). Chicago: University of Chicago Press, 1968.

Horne, Jo. *Caregiving: Helping an Aging Loved One.* Washington, DC: AARP Books, 1985.

Kagan, Robert. *The Evolving Self.* Cambridge, MA: Harvard University Press, 1982.

Kaplan, Louise J. *Adolescence: The Farewell To Childhood.* New York: Simon & Schuster, 1984.

Karpel, Mark A. *Family Resources.* New York: Guilford Press, 1986.

Keddie, Kenneth. *Action With the Elderly: A Handbook for Relatives and Friends.* New York: Peregon Press, 1978.

Kingson, Eric R., and Barbara A. Hirshorn and John M. Cornman. *Ties That Bind: The Interdependence of Generations.* Washington, DC: Seven Locks, 1986.

Kubler-Ross, Elisabeth. *On Death and Dying.* New York: McMillan, 1970.

Kuhlen, Raymond. "Developmental Changes in Motivation During the Adult Years." *Middle Age and Aging,* Neugarten (ed). Chicago: University of Chicago Press, 1968.

Lidoff, Lorraine. *Caregiver Support Groups in America.* Washington, DC: National Council on Aging, 1990.

Luft, Joseph, and Harry Ingham. *Of Human Interaction.* Mountain View, CA: Mayfield Publishing, 1969.

Maddox. *The Encyclopedia of Aging.* New York: Springer Publishing, 1987.

McRae, R.P. *Personality in Adulthood.* Boston: Little, Brown, 1984.

Mental Health Directory 1990. Washington, DC: National Institute of Mental Health, 1990.

Miller, Dorothy. "The Sandwich Generation: Adult Children of the Aging." *Social Work,* September 1981.

National Continuing Care Directory. Washington, DC: AARP Books, 1988.

National Directory of Retirement Facilities. Phoenix, AZ: Oryx Press, 1986.

Neugarten, Bernice. "Adult Personality: Toward a Psychology of the Life Cycle." *Middle Age and Aging,* Neugarten (ed). Chicago: University of Chicago Press, 1968.

Neugarten, Bernice. "The Awareness of Middle Age." *Middle Age and Aging,* Neugarten (ed); Chicago: University of Chicago Press, 1968.

Norris, Jane. *Daughters of the Elderly.* Bloomington, IN: Indiana University Press, 1988.

Peck, Robert. "Psychological Developments in the Second Half of Life." *Psychological Aspects of Aging,* John Anderson (ed). Washington, DC: American Psychological Association, 1956.

Portnow, Jay, and Martha Houtmann. *Home Care for the Elderly: A Complete Guide.* New York: McGraw-Hill, 1987.

Raper, Ann Trueblood. *National Continuing Care Directory.* Washington, DC: AARP Books, 1984.

Schcie, K.W., and J. Gewitz. *Adult Development and Aging.* Boston: Little, Brown, 1982.

Scott, L.E. "Caring For Your Aging Parents." *Healthy Living,* July 1990.

Selye, Hans. *The Stress of Life.* New York: McGraw-Hill, 1976.

Sheehy, Gail. *Passages.* New York: Dutton, 1976.

Silverstone, Barbara, and Helen Kendel Hyman. *You and Your Aging Parent.* New York: Random House, 1982.

Simos, Bertha G. *A Time to Grieve: Loss as a Universal Human Experience.* New York: Family Service Association of America, 1979.

Skala, Ken. *American Guidance for Those Over 60—Handbook of Benefits, Entitlements and Assistance.* Falls Church, VA: American Guidance, 1990.

Sommers, Tish, and Laurie Shields. *Women Take Care.* Gainsville, FL: Triad Publishing, 1987.

Steven-Long, Judith. *Adult Life: Developmental Processes.* Palo Alto, CA: Mayfield Publishing, 1979.

Walsh, Roma. "The Family in Later Life." *Journal of Gerontological Social Work*, June 1986.

Wasserman, Paul, and Barbara Koehler and Yvonne Lev. *Encyclopedia of Senior Citizen's Information Services.* Detroit, MI: Gale Research, 1986.

Wilson, Albert J.E. III. *Social Services for Older Persons.* Boston: Little, Brown, 1984.

Index